The CHOSEN

SEASON TWO

KIDS ACTIVITY BOOK

```
E
F      E
H      E
D  U V W
G I N T X K
N C M A A S S
T O N G A L U V
Q K Z N P K X A N C
A I L A R T S U A E A H
B I E U V V C Q K F M Z V G
O V R A I N O D E L A C W E N
C G U S D N A L S I K O O C E E H
A A E N I U G W E N U A P A P B N K
S O L O M O N I S L A N D S H N F I J I
           H
           N
D N A L S I S A M T S I R H C C C P D D
N E F R E N C H P O L Y N E S I A I A I
L P A O M A S N R E T S E W Q X
A I T A B I R I K A W A J F
```

BroadStreet
KIDS

BroadStreet Kids
Savage, Minnesota, USA

BroadStreet Kids is an imprint of BroadStreet Publishing®
Broadstreetpublishing.com

The
CHOSEN
Kids Activity Book: Season 2

978-1-4245-6488-0

Design by Chris Garborg | garborgdesign.com
Created, edited, and compiled by Michelle Winger | literallyprecise.com
Mazes licensed from mazegenerator.net.

Printed in China.

22 23 24 25 26 27 28   7 6 5 4 3 2 1

Alphabet practice!

Practice the first three letters of the Hebrew alphabet!

ALEF

This Hebrew letter is silent.

BET

This letter sounds like the **b** in boat.

GIMEL

This letter sounds like the **g** in goat.

FRESH MARKET

USE THE LETTERS AND NUMBERS
TO SHOW WHERE EACH OF THESE
PIECES BELONG IN THE PUZZLE.
WE GOT YOU STARTED! ⟶ A5

_____

_____

_____

_____

_____

_____

_____

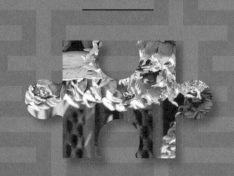

_____

_____

SECRET DECODER

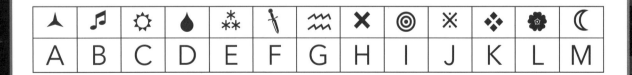

Use the code to
decipher the message
from Jesus' mother.

⚓	♫	☼	●	❄	🗡	〰	✖	◎	✳	❖	✿	☾
A	B	C	D	E	F	G	H	I	J	K	L	M

☸	⚑	🐕	◆	★	💰	✡	✝	⚷	🕊	●	□	✦
N	O	P	Q	R	S	T	U	V	W	X	Y	Z

See John 21:25.

7

Answer on page 150

CROSSWORD FUN

Use the clues to solve the crossword. Answers with two words are shown in parentheses telling how many letters are in each word.

ACROSS

3. The disciple who met Jesus on a construction set
6. The disciple who met Jesus when he was standing next to John the Baptist
7. The disciple who said he thought his career and reputation were going to be ruined before Jesus showed up
8. The woman who met Jesus for the first time in the tavern (4, 9)
11. The disciple who thought Jesus was a Roman when he first saw Him

DOWN

1. The disciple whose story about Jesus would have to be precise
2. The disciple who said, "He knew me before He knew me"
4. The disciple who said, "Come and see"
5. One of the disciples Jesus used to till and plant a field
9. The woman who treasured all the things of Jesus in her heart
10. The disciple who said Jesus loved him

MAZE

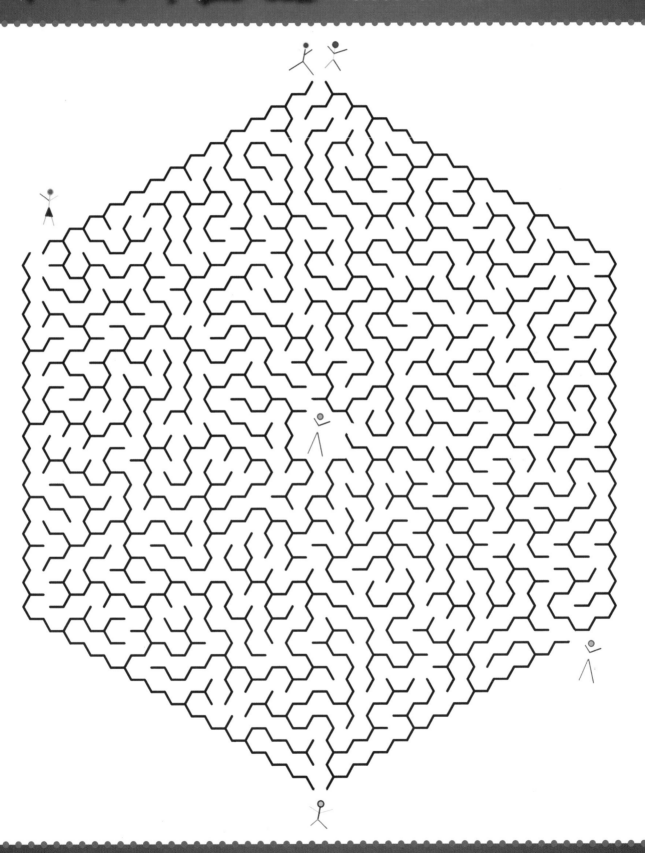

9

Word Search

Find the characters hidden in the word search puzzle.

ANDREW
BIG JAMES
DISHON
GERSHON
JESUS
JOHN
KAFNI
LITTLE JAMES
MARY MAGDALENE
MOTHER MARY
MATTHEW
MELECH
NATHANAEL
NEDIM
PHILIP
PHOTINA
RAMAH
SIMON
THADDEUS
THOMAS
TZURI

```
R  J  J  F  N  O  H  S  I  D  H  W  K  T  M
M  F  P  H  O  T  I  N  A  U  T  D  L  E  Y
S  Q  T  T  N  S  H  H  J  Z  R  L  S  B  R
P  T  I  H  S  O  T  V  U  O  I  L  A  I  A
H  W  J  R  A  G  H  R  Q  T  H  H  M  G  M
I  E  C  A  P  D  I  S  T  W  C  N  O  J  R
L  H  T  M  S  E  D  L  R  E  E  Z  H  A  E
I  T  M  A  C  I  E  E  L  E  R  Z  T  M  H
P  T  N  H  F  J  M  E  U  W  G  I  U  E  T
S  A  H  B  A  F  M  O  W  S  O  C  N  S  O
U  M  D  M  Z  X  V  J  N  J  R  L  P  P  M
S  L  E  I  N  A  T  H  A  N  A  E  L  N  E
E  S  N  D  A  F  G  A  W  E  R  D  N  A  S
J  E  N  E  L  A  D  G  A  M  Y  R  A  M  M
B  E  H  N  L  M  Q  K  A  F  N  I  Z  W  S
```

SHEEP COUNT

Find the 100 sheep
Jesus talked about
in His parable!

Start at the arrow and pass through groups of
sheep, collecting them as you go.

Find a path that adds up to exactly 100 sheep.

Only pass through a group of sheep once.

Groups must be directly connected (up-and-
down, side-to-side, and diagonally).

Each group that you collect must have at least
one black sheep in it.

100

Answer on page 150

WORD FIT

On the Road

Some of the places Jesus and His disciples planned to visit are listed below. These words only fit into the puzzle one way. Use the number of letters in each word as a clue to where it could be put. We have placed a word to help you get started.

5 LETTERS
JUDEA

6 LETTERS
HEBRON
JORDAN
MT EBAL
QUMRAN
SHILOH
SYCHAR

7 LETTERS
ANATOTH
EPHRAIM
GALILEE
JERICHO
SAMARIA
SEBASTE

8 LETTERS
NAZARETH

9 LETTERS
JERUSALEM
MT GERAZIM

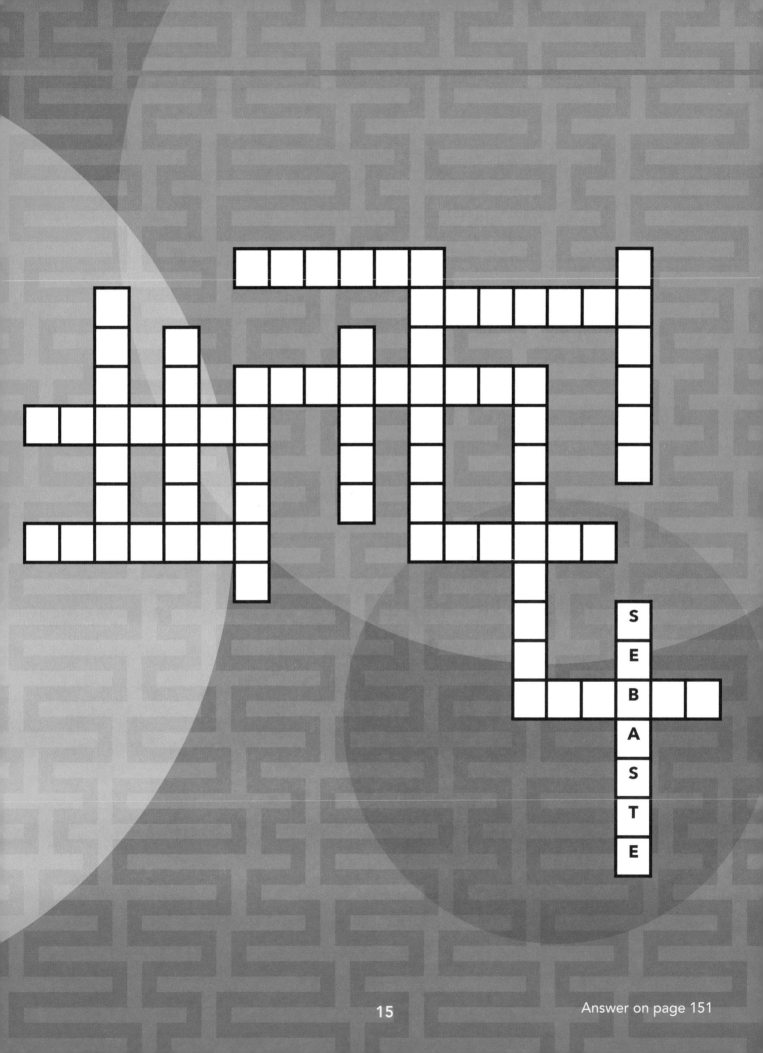

Answer on page 151

WORD IN WORD

Use the definitions to figure out the words. The letters in the small words will help you figure out the bigger words.

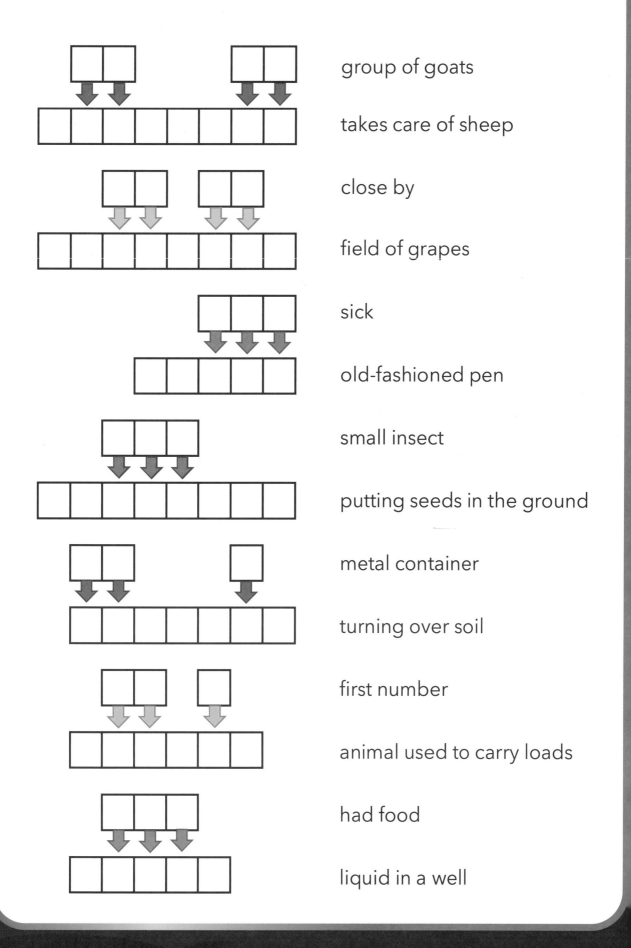

group of goats

takes care of sheep

close by

field of grapes

sick

old-fashioned pen

small insect

putting seeds in the ground

metal container

turning over soil

first number

animal used to carry loads

had food

liquid in a well

Answer on page 1

NUMBER

Jesus told a parable about leaving ninety-nine sheep to go find one lost sheep. He talked about how much the shepherd rejoices when the lost sheep is found! What did He say this meant for us?

Use the grid to figure out which letters go where, so you can read the answer. We have given you some numbers to start.

A	B	C	D	E	F	G	H	I	J	K	L	M
				3	26					20		

N	O	P	Q	R	S	T	U	V	W	X	Y	Z
4	18		25		5		24		16		23	

CODE

$\overline{5}$ $\overline{19}$ $\overline{3}$ $\overline{12}$ $\overline{3}$ $\quad$ $\overline{21}$ $\overline{8}$ $\overline{2}$ $\overline{2}$ $\quad$ $\overline{11}$ $\overline{3}$ $\quad$ $\overline{9}$ $\overline{18}$ $\overline{12}$ $\overline{3}$

$\overline{15}$ $\overline{18}$ $\overline{10}$ $\quad$ $\overline{8}$ $\overline{4}$ $\quad$ $\overline{19}$ $\overline{3}$ $\overline{6}$ $\overline{24}$ $\overline{3}$ $\overline{4}$ $\quad$ $\overline{18}$ $\overline{24}$ $\overline{3}$ $\overline{12}$

$\overline{18}$ $\overline{4}$ $\overline{3}$ $\quad$ $\overline{1}$ $\overline{8}$ $\overline{4}$ $\overline{4}$ $\overline{3}$ $\overline{12}$ $\quad$ $\overline{21}$ $\overline{19}$ $\overline{18}$

$\overline{12}$ $\overline{3}$ $\overline{7}$ $\overline{3}$ $\overline{4}$ $\overline{5}$ $\overline{1}$ $\quad$ $\overline{5}$ $\overline{19}$ $\overline{6}$ $\overline{4}$ $\quad$ $\overline{18}$ $\overline{24}$ $\overline{6}$ $\overline{12}$

$-$

$\overline{4}$ $\overline{8}$ $\overline{4}$ $\overline{3}$ $\overline{5}$ $\overline{10}$ $\quad$ $\overline{4}$ $\overline{8}$ $\overline{4}$ $\overline{3}$

$\overline{12}$ $\overline{8}$ $\overline{13}$ $\overline{19}$ $\overline{5}$ $\overline{3}$ $\overline{18}$ $\overline{14}$ $\overline{1}$ $\quad$ $\overline{21}$ $\overline{19}$ $\overline{18}$ $\quad$ $\overline{4}$ $\overline{3}$ $\overline{3}$ $\overline{17}$

$\cdot$

$\overline{4}$ $\overline{18}$ $\quad$ $\overline{12}$ $\overline{3}$ $\overline{7}$ $\overline{3}$ $\overline{4}$ $\overline{5}$ $\overline{6}$ $\overline{4}$ $\overline{22}$ $\overline{3}$

Read Matthew 18:10-14 or Luke 15:3-7.

Answer on page 151

JUMBLED WORDS

How long will the Word of God
be around?

Unscramble the words so you
can see what Jesus said to His
disciples about this.

E V E H A N   N A D

R A T H E   L I W L

A S P S   W A Y A '

U T B   Y M   S R W D O

T L L W   V E R N E

S A P S   Y A W A .

See Matthew 24:35.

Answer on page 151

Which Fish?

How did everything get here?

Each colored fish in the puzzle represents one of the five vowels: A, E, I, O, and U. Mark down which fish carries which vowel, and then write this popular Scripture in the space provided.

IN THE BEGINNING, GOD CREATED THE HEAVENS AND THE EARTH. THE EARTH WAS WITHOUT FORM AND VOID, AND DARKNESS WAS OVER THE FACE OF THE DEEP.

Read Genesis 1:1.

Answer on page 151

Which Spice?

GARLIC ONION PEPPER SALT

Follow the lines to figure out which
spice each of Jesus' followers
chose to flavor their food.
Write the name under the spice
in the space provided.

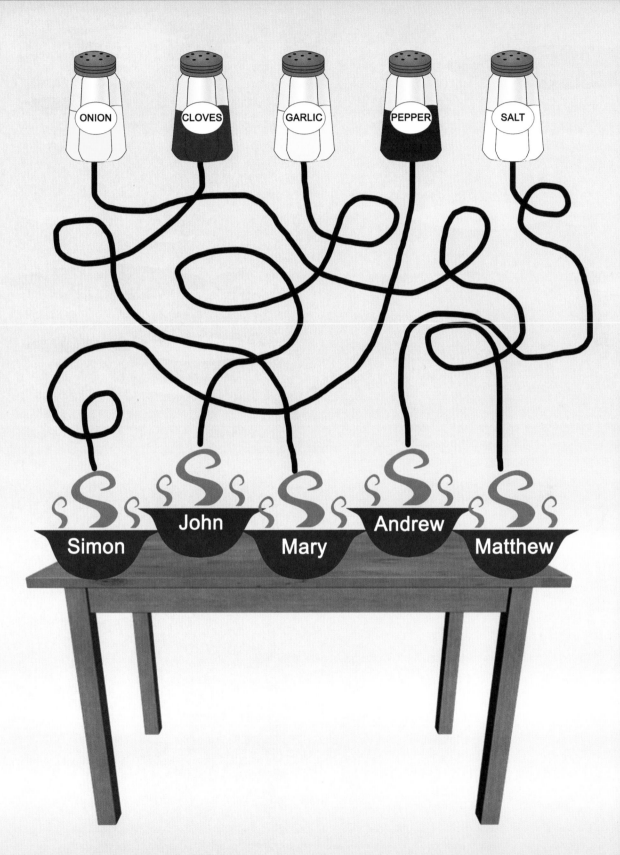

WORD CHANGE

Change the word SEED into TILL one letter at a time.

Use the clues to help you figure out each word.

S E E D

— — — —   unwanted plant

— — — —   join metal with heat

— — — —   raised bump on skin

— — — —   become liquid

— — — —   thick milkshake

— — — —   masculine gender

— — — —   distance

— — — —   type of flooring

T I L L

Alphabet practice!

Practice the next three letters of the Hebrew alphabet!

DALET

This letter sounds like the **d** in doll.

ד

HE

This letter sounds like the **h** in horse.

ה

WAW

This letter sounds like the **w** in well.

ו

GOLDEN DOOR

USE THE LETTERS AND NUMBERS
TO SHOW WHERE EACH OF THESE
PIECES BELONG IN THE PUZZLE.
WE GOT YOU STARTED! ⟶ F6

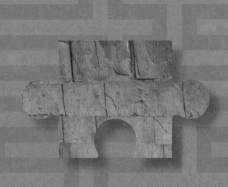

WORD FIT

Some of the people and places Jesus and His disciples saw are listed below. These words only fit into the puzzle one way. Use the number of letters in each word as a clue to where it could be put. We have placed a word for you to help you get started.

5 LETTERS
JONAH
SYRIA

6 LETTERS
BASHAN
FABIUS
MARCUS
MICHAL
TOBIAS

7 LETTERS
ANTIOCH
LEONTES
SAMARIA

8 LETTERS
DAMASCAS
SELEUCIA

9 LETTERS
BETHSAIDA
NATHANAEL
ZACHARIAH

16 LETTERS
CEASAREA
PHILIPPI

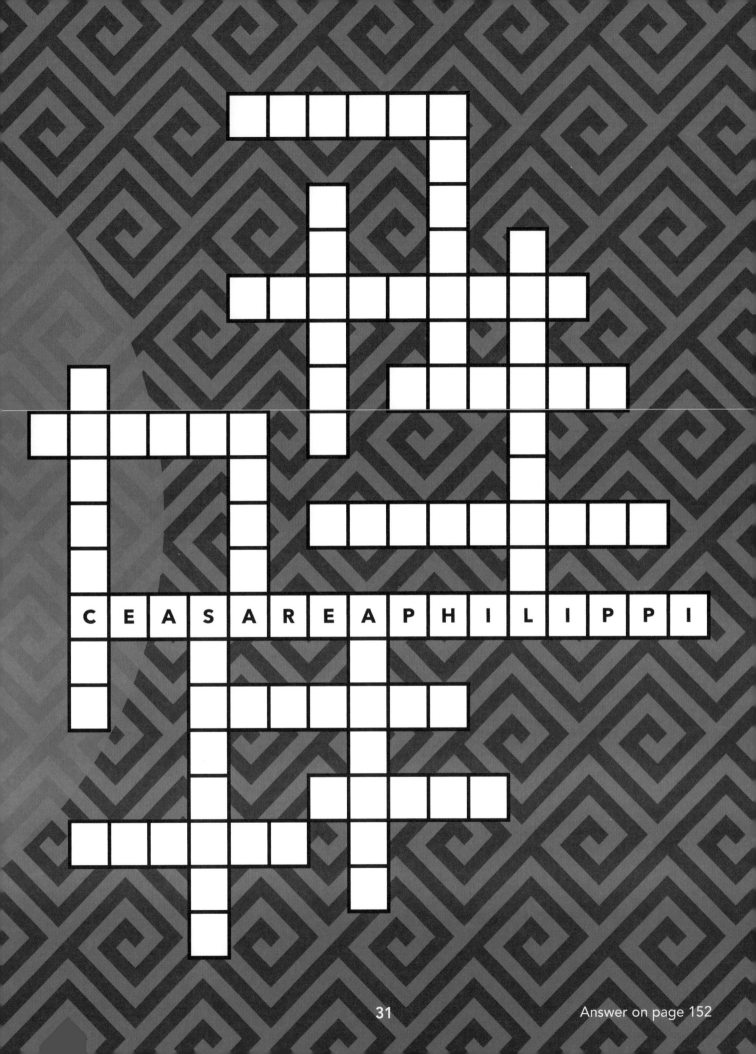

CEASAREAPHILIPPI

Answer on page 152

MYSTERY LETTERS

Using the color code, fill in the missing letters to see what Philip told Matthew about his identity. There are two mystery letters you will need to figure out to complete the message.

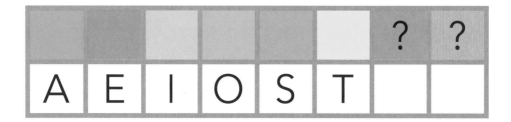

						?	?
A	E	I	O	S	T		

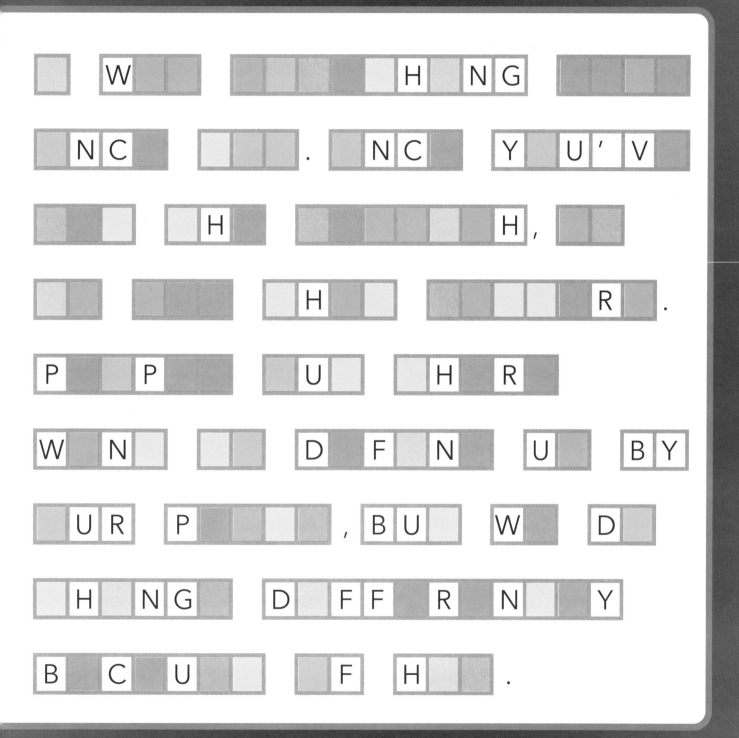

Answer on page 152

NUMBER CODE

Matthew didn't feel like he had everything he needed to follow Jesus.

Use the number grid to figure out which letters go where, so you can read what Philip said to Matthew.

A	B	C	D	E	F	G	H	I	J	K	L	M
5					23		4	24			11	

N	O	P	Q	R	S	T	U	V	W	X	Y	Z
9		20	13		16					18	12	

— —   — — — —   — — — — —
24 23   7 4 24 16   2 5 19 19 24

— — — — —   — — — —
17 15 16 22 16   23 2 6 14

— — — — — — — —   — — — — — —
9 5 25 5 2 15 7 4   8 5 11 11 15 1

— — — '   — —   — — — — —   — — —
12 6 22   24 7   14 15 5 9 16   12 6 22

— — — — — — —   — — — —
5 11 2 15 5 1 12   4 5 26 15

$\overline{15}$ $\overline{26}$ $\overline{15}$ $\overline{2}$ $\overline{12}$ $\overline{7}$ $\overline{4}$ $\overline{24}$ $\overline{9}$ $\overline{10}$ $\quad$ $\overline{12}$ $\overline{6}$ $\overline{22}$

$\overline{9}$ $\overline{15}$ $\overline{15}$ $\overline{1}$ $\quad$ $\overline{23}$ $\overline{6}$ $\overline{2}$ $\quad$ $\overline{2}$ $\overline{24}$ $\overline{10}$ $\overline{4}$ $\overline{7}$

$\overline{9}$ $\overline{6}$ $\overline{3}$ $'$ $\overline{5}$ $\overline{9}$ $\overline{1}$ $\quad$ $\overline{4}$ $\overline{15}$ $\quad$ $\overline{3}$ $\overline{24}$ $\overline{11}$ $\overline{11}$

$\overline{10}$ $\overline{24}$ $\overline{26}$ $\overline{15}$ $\quad$ $\overline{12}$ $\overline{6}$ $\overline{22}$ $\quad$ $\overline{7}$ $\overline{4}$ $\overline{15}$

$\overline{2}$ $\overline{15}$ $\overline{16}$ $\overline{7}$ $\quad$ $\overline{24}$ $\overline{9}$ $\quad$ $\overline{7}$ $\overline{24}$ $\overline{14}$ $\overline{15}$ $\cdot$

$\overline{3}$ $\overline{4}$ $\overline{5}$ $\overline{7}$ $\quad$ $\overline{12}$ $\overline{6}$ $\overline{22}$ $\quad$ $\overline{7}$ $\overline{4}$ $\overline{24}$ $\overline{9}$ $\overline{21}$

$\overline{12}$ $\overline{6}$ $\overline{22}$ $\quad$ $\overline{21}$ $\overline{9}$ $\overline{6}$ $\overline{3}$ $\quad$ $\overline{1}$ $\overline{6}$ $\overline{15}$ $\overline{16}$ $\overline{9}$ $'$ $\overline{7}$

$\overline{14}$ $\overline{5}$ $\overline{7}$ $\overline{7}$ $\overline{15}$ $\overline{2}$ $'$ $\overline{6}$ $\overline{9}$ $\overline{11}$ $\overline{12}$ $\quad$ $\overline{7}$ $\overline{4}$ $\overline{5}$ $\overline{7}$

$\overline{17}$ $\overline{15}$ $\overline{16}$ $\overline{22}$ $\overline{16}$ $\quad$ $\overline{8}$ $\overline{4}$ $\overline{6}$ $\overline{16}$ $\overline{15}$ $\quad$ $\overline{12}$ $\overline{6}$ $\overline{22}$ $\cdot$

$\overline{7}$ $\overline{4}$ $\overline{5}$ $\overline{7}$ $\quad$ $\overline{16}$ $'$ $\overline{3}$ $\overline{4}$ $\overline{15}$ $\overline{2}$ $\overline{15}$

$\overline{12}$ $\overline{6}$ $\overline{22}$ $\overline{2}$ $\quad$ $\overline{8}$ $\overline{6}$ $\overline{9}$ $\overline{23}$ $\overline{24}$ $\overline{1}$ $\overline{15}$ $\overline{9}$ $\overline{8}$ $\overline{15}$

$\overline{8}$ $\overline{6}$ $\overline{14}$ $\overline{15}$ $\overline{16}$ $\quad$ $\overline{23}$ $\overline{2}$ $\overline{6}$ $\overline{14}$ $\quad$ $\overline{9}$ $\overline{6}$ $\overline{3}$ $\cdot$

35

Answer on page 152

PATH WORDS

Beginning with the yellow star and ending with the red stop sign, connect the houses to re-create Nathanael's prayer to God.

Each house with a word must be visited once. Empty houses should not be visited. The words can only connect along the paths (side-to-side and up-and-down).

There are a few clues here to help you choose the right path. Write the missing words as you go along.

HEAR _____ _____ _____ _____;

LET _____ _____ _____ _____

_____. DO _____ _____ _____

FACE_____ _____ _____ _____

_____ _____ MY _____. _____

YOUR _____ _____ _____; _____

_____ _____ IN _____ _____

_____ _____ CALL.

Answer on page 152

Which Fish?

Each colored fish in the puzzle represents a letter (all five vowels and two consonants). Figure out which fish carries which letter, and then write Ramah's prayer of thanks in the space.

_____

_____

_____

_____

_____

_____

_____

TH◯◯KF◯L
B◯F◯R◯ Y◯◯, L◯V◯◯G
◯D ◯◯D R◯◯G
K◯◯G, F◯R Y◯◯ H◯V◯
◯RC◯F◯LLY
R◯ST◯R◯D ◯Y S◯◯L
W◯TH◯◯ ◯◯.
GR◯◯T ◯S Y◯◯R
F◯◯THF◯L◯◯SS.

SECRET DECODER

Use the code to decipher a message from Jesus to one of His disciples.
Write down the letters in the boxes to find out which disciple Jesus was talking to.

☀	♫	☼	◗	✳	⚔	≈	✖	◎	✦	❖	✿	☾
A	B	C	D	E	F	G	H	I	J	K	L	M

☸	⚑	🐈	◆	★	💰	✡	✝	⚷	🕊	●	◻	✦
N	O	P	Q	R	S	T	U	V	W	X	Y	Z

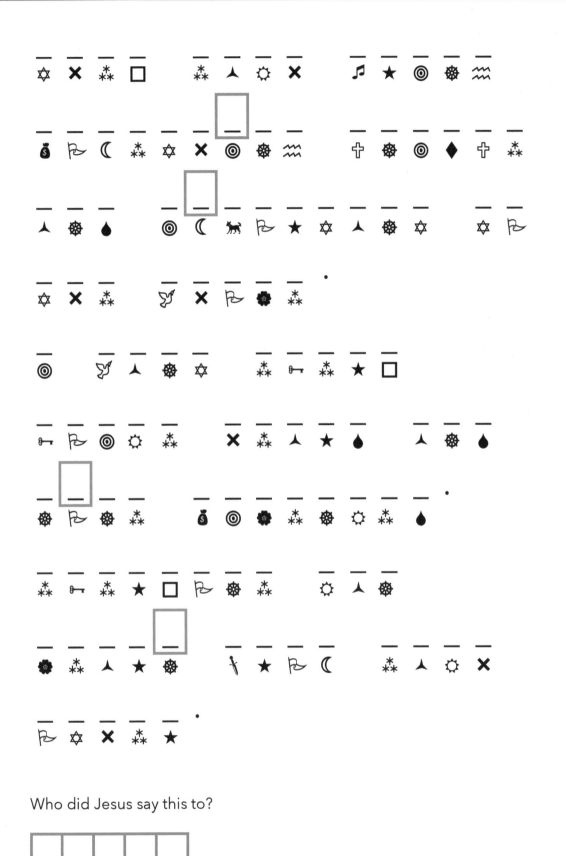

Who did Jesus say this to?

Answer on page 153

WORD CHANGE

Change the word PLAN into HOME one letter at a time.

Use the clues to help you figure out each word.

P L A N

_ _ _ _   family or group

_ _ _ _   smack hands together

_ _ _ _   move arms like a bird

_ _ _ _   level or smooth

_ _ _ _   achievement

_ _ _ _   party or gathering

_ _ _ _   very quick

_ _ _ _   already happened

_ _ _ _   stick for a sign

_ _ _ _   position yourself for a photo

_ _ _ _   long tube for spraying water

H O M E

Practice the next three letters of the Hebrew alphabet!

ZAYIN

This letter sounds like the **z** in Zebedee.

ז

HET

This letter sounds like the **ch** in Bach.

ח

TET

This letter sounds like the **t** in tax.

ט

PATIO PUZZLE

USE THE LETTERS AND NUMBERS
TO SHOW WHERE EACH OF THESE
PIECES BELONG IN THE PUZZLE.
WE GOT YOU STARTED! —————→ E7

_____

_____

_____

_____

_____

_____

_____

_____

_____

LETTER DROP

Use the definitions to figure out the words. The letters with arrows "drop" down into the boxes below them to help you complete each word.

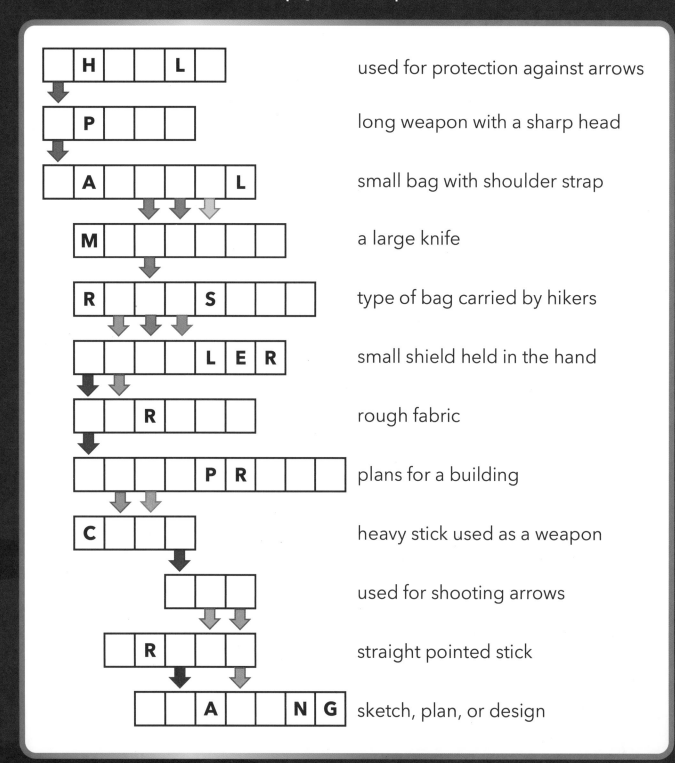

| | H | | L | | used for protection against arrows |

| | P | | | | long weapon with a sharp head |

| | A | | | | | L | small bag with shoulder strap |

| M | | | | | | | a large knife |

| R | | | S | | | type of bag carried by hikers |

| | | | | L | E | R | small shield held in the hand |

| | R | | | | rough fabric |

| | | | | P | R | | | | plans for a building |

| C | | | | heavy stick used as a weapon |

| | | | | used for shooting arrows |

| | R | | | straight pointed stick |

| | | A | | | N | G | sketch, plan, or design |

PICTURE MESSAGE

Use the pictures to help you figure out what Jesus said to Philip about friends.

 – CL – F

 – BE + W

_____

 – OR

 – K

_____

 – C + M

_____

4

_____

 – BE + W

 – H + W

_____

 – K

 – I + A

_____

– T + Y

_____ .

Answer on page 153

Word Search

Find these typical jobs hidden in the word search puzzle.

ARCHITECT

BRICK LAYER

CARPENTER

CRAFTSMAN

FARMER

FISHERMAN

FOREMAN

INNKEEPER

PRIEST

RABBI

SCRIBE

TAX COLLECTOR

TEACHER

TRADER

TREASURER

VINTNER

```
                              I
                          R   D   L
                      R   C   Z   R   P
                  E   O   B   K   Q   R   A
              H   R   A   B   B   I   I   T   V
          C   A   J   I   U   K   B   E   Z   C   C
      A   V   O   T   E   U   P   R   S   Q   R   A   E
  E   I   Z   C   X   X   I   D   U   T   Y   T   R   Q   I
  T   A   X   C   O   L   L   E   C   T   O   R   P   P   Y   J   L
  I   A   R   C   H   I   T   E   C   T   U   N   A   M   E   R   O   F   U
W D B W F R E G A N R K N U X N C J D N B
      W   T   I           Y   U   I               T   B   R
      P   R   E           O   M   T               E   R   P
      A   E   C           O   T   L               R   I   I
      A   A   I           X   K   K               W   C   O
      U   S   Q   R   I   N   N   K   E   E   P   E   R   K   A
      R   U   P   E   N   A   M   S   T   F   A   R   C   L   Y
      F   R   W   M   M   M   H   V   V   S   K   E   U   A   D
      T   E   Y   R   N   R               I   K   A   F   Y   N
      Q   R   E   A   K   E               Z   N   Q   A   E   H
      F   B   W   F   M   H               U   W   T   O   R   V
      E   B   I   R   C   S               E   Z   B   N   H   D
      C   W   E   G   V   I               T   R   A   D   E   R
      V   J   R   H   R   F               L   E   O   M   D   R
```

49

LETTER WHEEL

Use the letters in the wheel to complete Jesus' message to Nathanael. Letters can be used multiple times.

A E F H I N O

D_ _'T L_ _K _T _ _M,
L_ _K _T M_.
W_ _ _ Y_U W_R_ _ _
Y_UR L_W_ST M_M_ _T,
_ _D Y_U W_R_ _L_ _ _,
_ D_D _ _T TUR_ MY
_ _C_ _R_M Y_U.
_ S_W Y_U.

Answer on page 153

WORD PIECES

The words for the answers to the questions below have fallen apart. Piece them back together to find the answers. Each group of letters should only be used once.

ES HAN NAZ MAT NAT

FIG THIR TEEN PHI TH

LIP TREE RA MAH AND

AEL ARE THEW BIG

TO REW RAH JAM

1. What age was Matthew when he bought his first house? (8 letters)

_____

2. What was Nathanael sitting under? (3 letters, 4 letters)

_____

3. Which disciple was sent to Jesus from John the Baptist? (6 letters)

_____

4. Who was Mary teaching to read and write? (5 letters)

_____

5. Which disciple was labeled the truth-teller? (9 letters)

_____

6. Which city did the disciples say nothing good could come out of? (8 letters)

_____

7. What disciple was found writing down everything Jesus did? (7 letters)

_____

8. Who had the longest shift pulling the cart? (3 letters, 5 letters)

_____

9. Who did Philip say John the Baptist was proud of? (6 letters)

_____

10. What were Matthew, Mary, and Ramah studying? (5 letters)

_____

Answer on page 153

MAZE

Find Nathanael
under the fig tree!

Start
here

WORD (IN) WORD

Use the definitions to figure out the words. The letters in the small words will help you figure out the bigger words. We have started the first one for you.

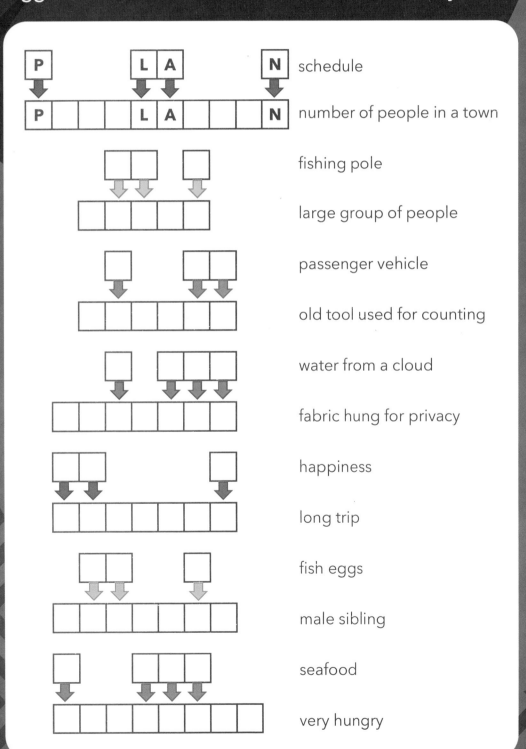

P　　L A　　N	schedule
P　　L A　　N	number of people in a town
	fishing pole
	large group of people
	passenger vehicle
	old tool used for counting
	water from a cloud
	fabric hung for privacy
	happiness
	long trip
	fish eggs
	male sibling
	seafood
	very hungry

Answer on page 153

Logic Grid

Uh-oh! Matthew is trying to organize the cart-pulling schedule, but the information he wrote down is just a mess of notes. Help Matthew sort through his notes, so he can figure out who pulled the cart when.

Use the grid to help you make sense of the jumbled information.

CLUES

- 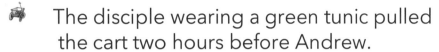 The disciple wearing a green tunic pulled the cart two hours before Andrew.
- Big James pulled the cart later than John.
- Big James was wearing a brown tunic.
- The disciple wearing a blue tunic pulled the cart at 8:00am.
- The disciple who pulled the cart at 10:00am was either wearing brown or he was Andrew.

		TUNIC COLOR				TIME			
		BLUE	BROWN	YELLOW	GREEN	8:00	10:00	12:00	2:00
DISCIPLE	BIG JAMES								
	ANDREW								
	SIMON								
	JOHN								
TIME	8:00 AM								
	10:00 AM								
	12:00 PM								
	2:00 PM								

Answer on page 153

Alphabet practice!

Practice the next three letters of the Hebrew alphabet!

YOD

This letter sounds like the **y** in you.

KAF

This letter sounds like the **k** in key.

LAMED

This letter sounds like the **l** in love.

WORD CHANGE

Answer on page 154

Change the word SINS into HOLY one letter at a time. Use the clues to help you figure out each word.

S I N S

_ _ _ _ metal containers

_ _ _ _ a lot

_ _ _ _ shirts

_ _ _ _ small jumps

_ _ _ _ believe for good things

_ _ _ _ hollow place

H O L Y

Group the Sick

Help the disciples group people together so they can bring them to Jesus. They must be placed in groups of ten and every group must have five 👧 and five 👦 when combined.

Write the letter pairs here.

_____   _____

_____   _____

_____   _____

_____   _____

_____   _____

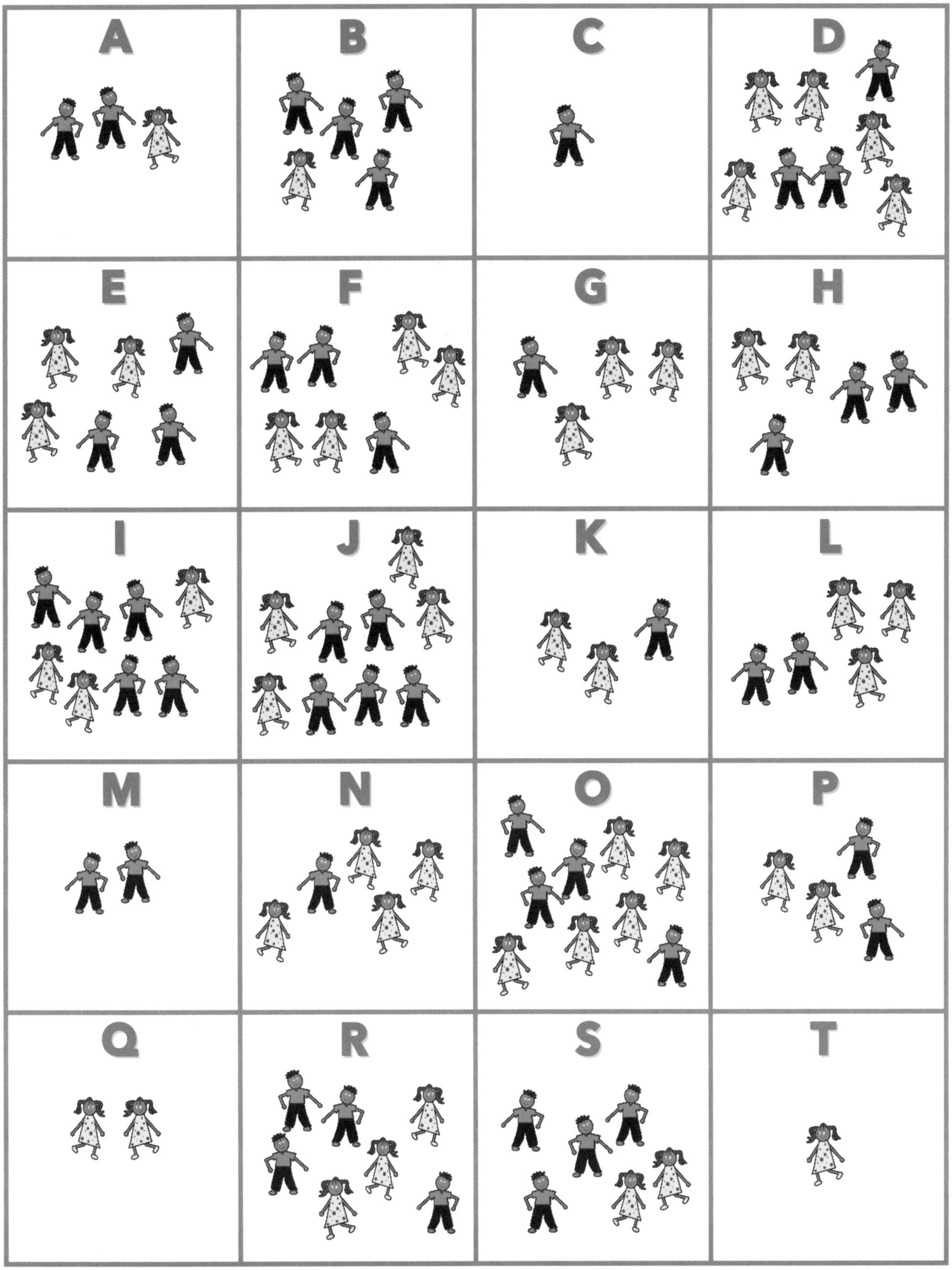
A
B
C
D
E
F
G
H
I
J
K
L
M
N
O
P
Q
R
S
T

MYSTERY LETTERS

Using the color code, fill in the missing letters to see what Philip said to Matthew about getting close to God. There are two mystery letters you will need to figure out to complete the message.

					?	?
A	E	I	O	U		

LETTER WHEEL

Use the letters in the wheel to complete the psalm Matthew was learning. Letters can be used multiple times.

_F _ _SC_ _D T_

H_ _V_ _, YOU _R_

_H_ R _. _F _ M_K_

MY B_D _ _ _H_

D_ P_HS, YOU _R_

_H_ R_.

See Psalm 139:8.

Answer on page 154

NUMBER CODE

Mary had a great message to share with the other disciples.

Use the grid to figure out which letters go where, so you can read what she said. We have given you some numbers to begin.

A	B	C	D	E	F	G	H	I	J	K	L	M
12							9		3			

N	O	P	Q	R	S	T	U	V	W	X	Y	Z
		8	24		10		26	1		6		19

11 _ _ 18 20 13 _ 23 _ 23 9 11 13 14 ʼ

9 2 _ 10 _ 15 12 11 23 11 13 16 ʼ

22 20 4 _ 26 10 _ 23 20 _ 21 2

9 20 25 17 .

11 _ 23 9 11 13 14 _ 9 2 _ 10 ʼ

9 2 4 2 _ 21 2 5 12 26 10 2

15 2 _ 5 12 13 _ 23 _ 21 2 ʼ

9 20 25 17 _ 15 11 23 9 20 26 23

9 11 7 .

Answer on page 154

MATCH UP

Match the people on the right
with their descriptions on the left.

Said he wouldn't mind being famous	ANDREW
Took and ate pork once	MATTHEW
Stayed in the tent healing all day	LITTLE JAMES
Said she always did what she was told	JOHN
Could recite half the Torah and loved the rules	SIMON
Had a form of paralysis	RAMAH
Ate meat with cheese once	BIG JAMES
Left everything when she lost a parent	MOTHER MARY
Washed Jesus' feet after a long day of ministry	THADDEUS
Said he would never forgive Matthew for his betrayal	THOMAS
A rule-follower from birth	MARY MAGDALENE
Had a lot of money before following Jesus	JESUS

Answer on page 154

Help the sick people find Jesus.

Word Search

Find all the words in the word search and then put them in order so you can read the prayer Jesus said before He went to bed after a busy day of healing people.

ARE
BLESSED
BRINGS
EYES
GOD
KING
LORD
MY
OF
OUR
SLEEP
THE
TO
UNIVERSE
WHO
YOU

T D E S S E L B

P O Y Q F U S

Q G O O X N

O O U E L F

D U E S D

S U R L Z

G N Q E S

N I L E E

I V P P Y

R E K P E

B R H A Y

H S R T Y L

E G N I K O

F D W H O R A

L X I N D Y M M

_ _ _ _ _ _ _ _ _ _ _ _/

_ _ _ _ _ _ _ _ _ _/

_ _ _ _ _ _ _ _ _

_ _ _ _ _ _ _/ _ _ _

_ _ _ _ _ _ _ _ _ _ _ _

_ _ _ _ _ _ _ _.

SECRET DECODER

Use the code to read a
message Simon spoke.
Note the letters in the boxes
to figure out what he was
talking about.

⚓	♫	☼	⬤	✳	🗡	〰	✖	◎	※	❖	✿	☾
A	B	C	D	E	F	G	H	I	J	K	L	M

☸	⚑	🐈	◆	★	💰	✡	✝	🗝	🕊	●	▢	✦
N	O	P	Q	R	S	T	U	V	W	X	Y	Z

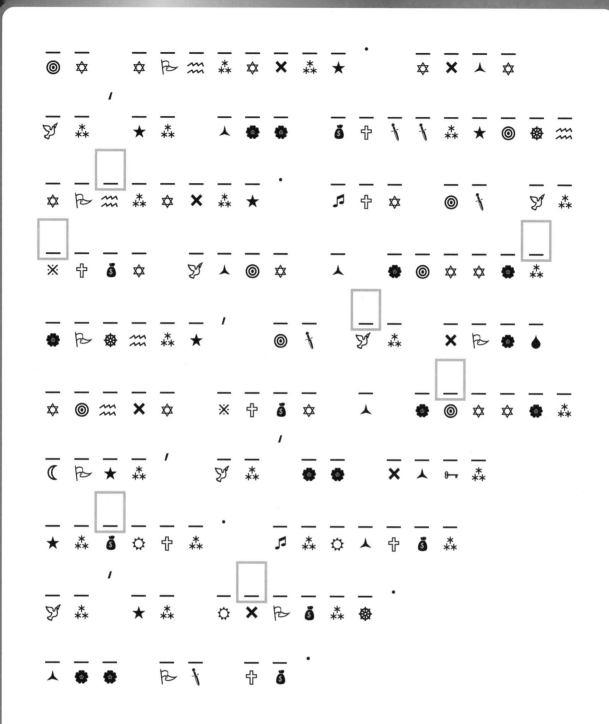

What was Simon talking about?

Alphabet practice!

Practice the next three letters of the Hebrew alphabet!

MEM

This letter sounds like the **m** in market.

NUN

This letter sounds like the **n** in net.

SAMEKH

This letter sounds like the **s** in sea.

SPICE IT UP

USE THE LETTERS AND NUMBERS
TO SHOW WHERE EACH OF THESE
PIECES BELONG IN THE PUZZLE.
WE GOT YOU STARTED! ⟶ D8

_____

_____

_____

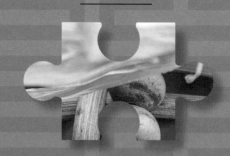

_____

_____

_____

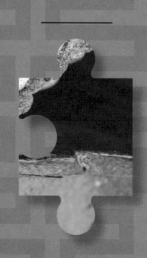

_____

_____

_____

Answer on page 154

WORD FIT

Here are some more locations that Jesus and His disciples may have encountered. These words only fit into the puzzle one way. Use the number of letters in each word as a clue to where it could be put.

6 LETTERS
SUKKAH

7 LETTERS
DEAD SEA

9 LETTERS
AGORA GATE
ARCH ALLEY
CATACOMBS
LOWER CITY
UPPER CITY

10 LETTERS
PRAETORIUM
WILDERNESS

11 LETTERS
TEMPLE MOUNT

12 LETTERS
HEBRON MARKET

13 LETTERS
DESERT PLATEAU
SOLOMON'S PORCH

14 LETTERS
POOL OF BETHESDA

15 LETTERS
ANTONIA FORTRESS

Answer on page 155

Word Search

Find all the characters in the word search.

ATTICUS	OCTAVIA
AXIUS	PETRONIUS
CAIPHAS	RUFUS
HONI	SHMUEL
ITHRAN	SIMON Z
JESSE	YANNI
LINUS	ZEBULON
MENACHEM	ZEPHANIAH

```
            C B Z D J P I V
          L K Y I W H L E M L J D
        Q N P T O S O P T D J L F P
        Q G N H   H O G R   E Q U V
      A F S R T   M X Z O   D S R M Z
      U X A W K   U O S N   T D S M E
    X Y N I B Z   E S H I   J J H E P M
    P R S F U O   L A T U   V O Y X H N
    F O G I V S   U H Y S   N N N C A I
    Z E B U L O N I Y P D K U I R I S Q N C
    S S X D V X J V A I V A T C O U U M I R
    G M N X I F Q M P A C W X D F V F U A K
    S I E   G O I O H C D L S U Y Z   U H M
    B S N   W U X J J I H R B Q     U K Z
    K G N   M E N A C H E M       N P N
    H Y S A                   X E L L
    S M L Y                 I S I W
      G A Q W Y B O V S Z Z O N C
      A T T I C U S B R N U S
        I S I M O N Z S
```

MATCH UP

Match the people with their descriptions. In the little boxes, write the letter of the description that best matches the person pictured.

I can enter the Holy of Holies.	I help my master.	I move from place to place a lot.	I am a follower of Jesus.
I keep the sheep together in the right place.	I am a new member of a group.	I protect one person at a time.	I am a native to my region.
I am very passionate about my religion.	I teach in the synagogue.	I sell things.	I am a spectator.
I buy things.	I work my land so I can grow and harvest crops.	I am the commander of a large company of men.	I am learning how to do my new job.
I do physical work.	I am guilty of breaking the law.	I fight in an army.	I am an elected official of the law.

☐ SOLDIER	☐ BODYGUARD	☐ TRAINEE	☐ CENTURION
☐ VENDOR	☐ CITIZEN	☐ ONLOOKER	☐ TRAVELER
☐ RABBI	☐ HIGH PRIEST	☐ ZEALOT	☐ RECRUIT
☐ SERVANT	☐ FARMER	☐ CRIMINAL	☐ HERDER
☐ MAGISTRATE	☐ DISCIPLE	☐ LABORER	☐ CUSTOMER

Answer on page 155

Which Fish?

Each colored fish in the puzzle represents a letter (all five vowels and two consonants). Figure out which fish carries which letter, and then read this Scripture passage found in Zephaniah.

F◦R N◦◦, ◦, Z◦◦N; L◦◦

N◦◦ Y◦◦R H◦ND◦ GR◦W

W◦◦K. ◦H◦ L◦RD Y◦◦R

G◦D ◦◦ ◦N Y◦◦R

M◦D◦◦, ◦ M◦◦GH◦Y ◦N◦

WH◦ W◦LL ◦◦V◦. H◦

W◦LL R◦J◦◦C◦ ◦V◦R

Y◦◦ W◦◦H GL◦DN◦◦◦;

84

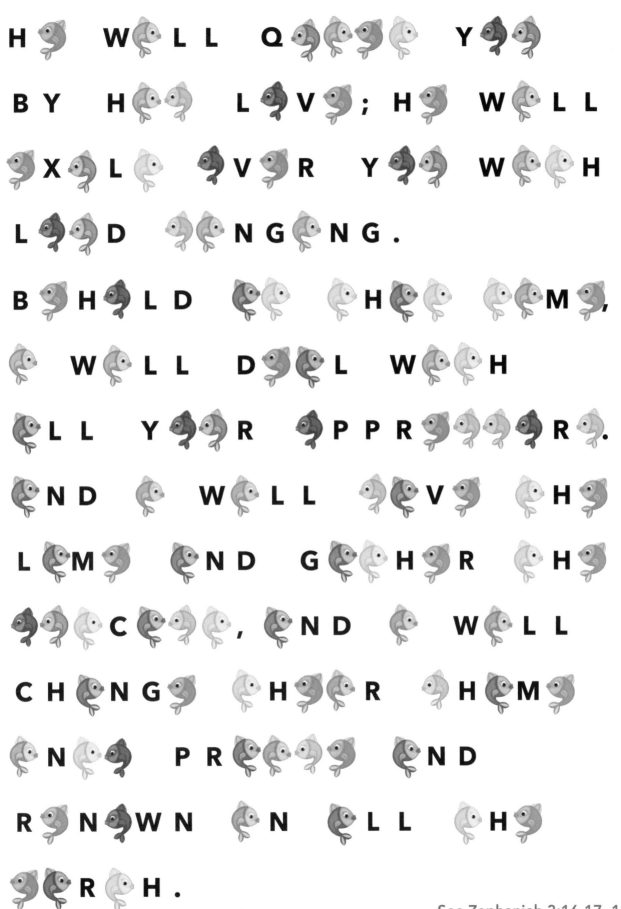

See Zephaniah 3:16-17, 19.

Answer on page 155

SECRET DECODER

Use the code to read a question that Big James asked Jesus.
Use the numbers under the letters to solve the
second coded message and discover Jesus' answer.

⚲	♪	✺	◗	✳	🗡	≋	✖	◎	✳	❖	✿	☾
A	B	C	D	E	F	G	H	I	J	K	L	M

✸	⚑	🐈	◆	★	💰	✡	✝	⚷	🕊	●	◻	✦
N	O	P	Q	R	S	T	U	V	W	X	Y	Z

How did Jesus answer this?

— — — — — — — —   — — —
1 2 3 4 5 6 7 8   9 10 11

— — — — — — — —   — —   — — —
12 13 14 15 16 17 18 19   20 21   22 23 24

— — — — — — — — — —   — —
25 26 27 28 29 30 31 32 33 34   35 36

— — — —   — — — — —   .
37 38 39 40   41 42 43 44 45

Answer on page 155

Find the 20 drops of water hidden in the sukkah.

"If a few raindrops get through, it's a reminder of our dependence on God, of His provision, and of how our people were so vulnerable in the wilderness. And He brought us through." —Mary Magdalene

PICTURE MESSAGE

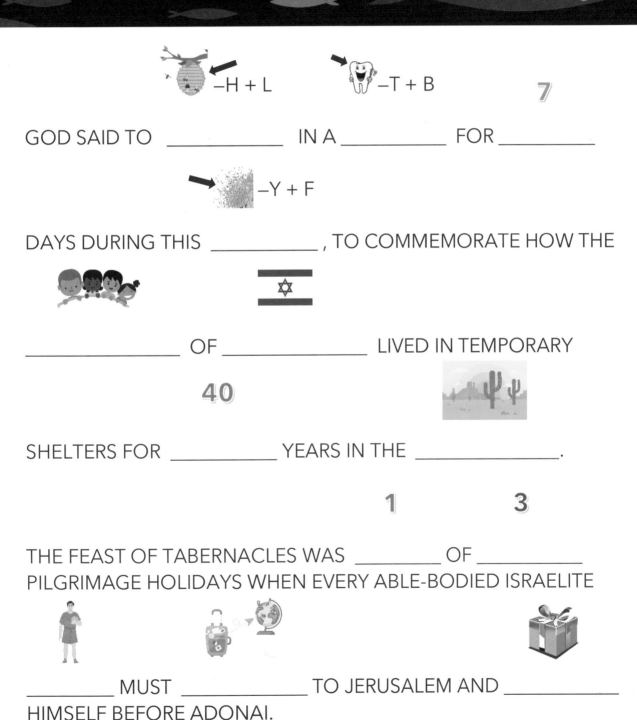

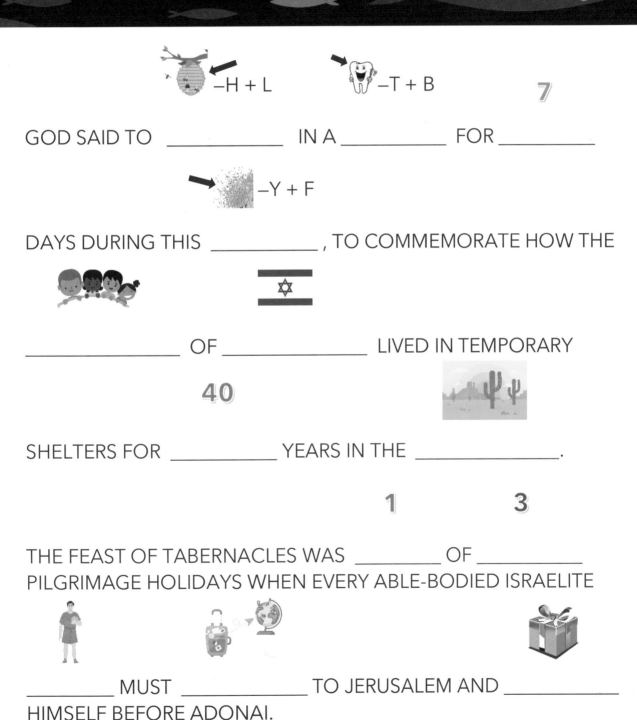–H + L   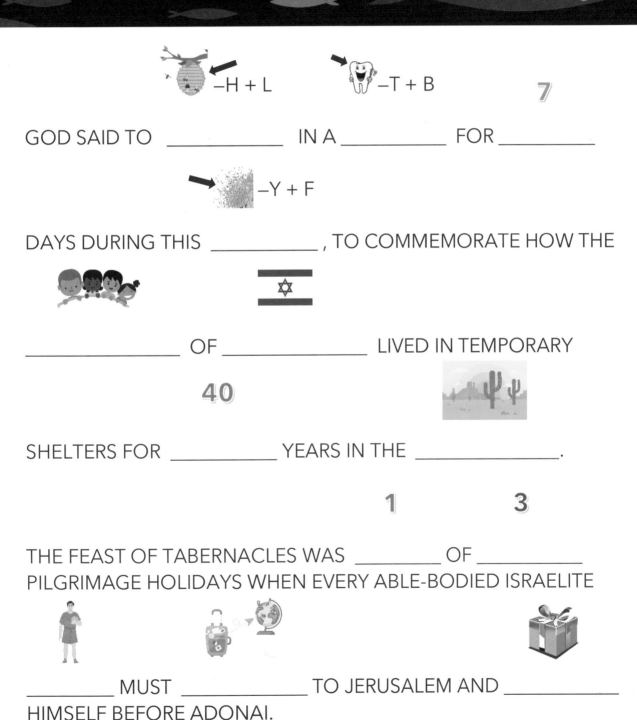–T + B   **7**

GOD SAID TO _____ IN A _____ FOR _____

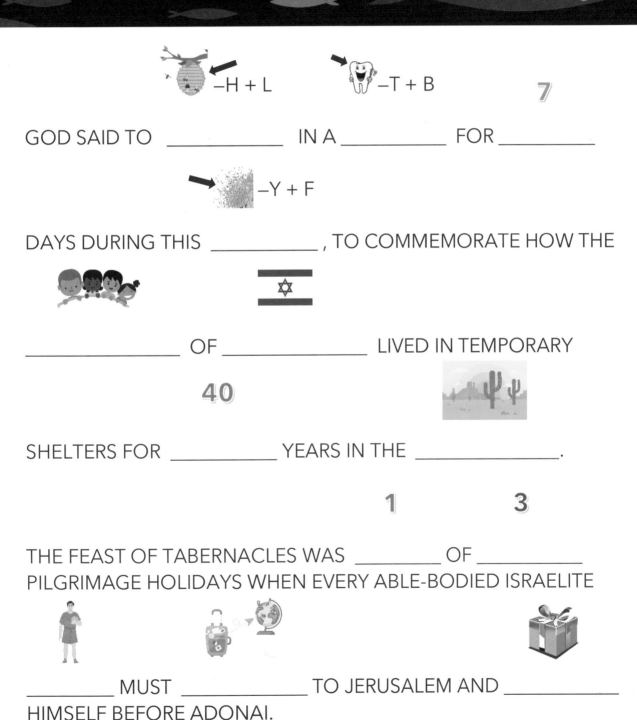–Y + F

DAYS DURING THIS _____ , TO COMMEMORATE HOW THE

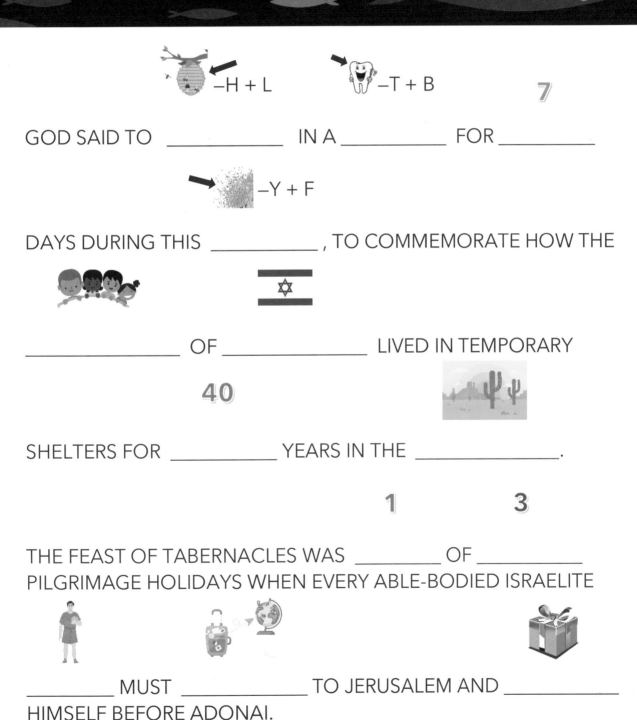

_____ OF _____ LIVED IN TEMPORARY

40

SHELTERS FOR _____ YEARS IN THE _____.

1   **3**

THE FEAST OF TABERNACLES WAS _____ OF _____
PILGRIMAGE HOLIDAYS WHEN EVERY ABLE-BODIED ISRAELITE

_____ MUST _____ TO JERUSALEM AND _____
HIMSELF BEFORE ADONAI.

NUMBER CODE

Jesus spoke powerful words to the crippled man at the Pool of Bethesda.

Use the grid to figure out which letters go where, so you can read what He said to Jesse. We have given you some numbers to begin.

A	B	C	D	E	F	G	H	I	J	K	L	M
8				4				5	23			

N	O	P	Q	R	S	T	U	V	W	X	Y	Z
14	3		19		9	7	24		26			22

'
__ __ __ __ __ __ __ __ __ __ __
5   6   14 3   9   8 11 16 5 14 2

'
__ __ __ __ __ __ __ __ __ __ __ __ __ __ __ __ __
8 18 3   7   9   21 25 3   11   25 4 10 13 5 14 2

__ __ __ __ __ __ __ __ __ __ __ '
3   1   14 3   9   25 4 10 13 5 14 2

'
__ __ __ __ __ __ __ __ __ __ __ __ __ ...
21 25 3   11   5 14   17 3   7   1   21 8 17

$\overline{5}'$ $\overline{6}$ $\overline{8}$ $\overline{11}$ $\overline{16}$ $\overline{5}$ $\overline{14}$ $\overline{2}$ $\overline{8}$ $\overline{18}$ $\overline{3}$ $\overline{7}$ $\overline{9}$

$\overline{17}$ $\overline{3}$ $\overline{7}$. $\overline{17}$ $\overline{3}$ $\overline{7}$ $\overline{15}$ $\overline{3}$ $\overline{14}$ $\overline{9}'$ $\overline{21}$ $\overline{8}$ $\overline{14}$ $\overline{9}$

$\overline{20}$ $\overline{8}$ $\overline{10}$ $\overline{11}$ $\overline{4}$ $\overline{25}$ $\overline{3}$ $\overline{13}$ $\overline{4}$ $\overline{8}$ $\overline{2}$ $\overline{8}$ $\overline{5}$ $\overline{14}'$ $\overline{5}$

$\overline{7}$ $\overline{14}$ $\overline{15}$ $\overline{4}$ $\overline{1}$ $\overline{11}$ $\overline{9}$ $\overline{8}$ $\overline{14}$ $\overline{15}$. $\overline{18}$ $\overline{7}$ $\overline{9}$

$\overline{9}$ $\overline{25}$ $\overline{5}$ $\overline{11}$ $\overline{13}$ $\overline{3}$ $\overline{3}$ $\overline{10}$ $\overline{25}$ $\overline{8}$ $\overline{11}$

$\overline{14}$ $\overline{3}$ $\overline{9}$ $\overline{25}$ $\overline{5}$ $\overline{14}$ $\overline{2}$ $\overline{20}$ $\overline{3}$ $\overline{1}$ $\overline{17}$ $\overline{3}$ $\overline{7}$; $\overline{5}$ $\overline{9}$

$\overline{6}$ $\overline{4}$ $\overline{8}$ $\overline{14}$ $\overline{11}$ $\overline{14}$ $\overline{3}$ $\overline{9}$ $\overline{25}$ $\overline{5}$ $\overline{14}$ $\overline{2}'$ $\overline{8}$ $\overline{14}$ $\overline{15}$

$\overline{17}$ $\overline{3}$ $\overline{7}$ $\overline{16}$ $\overline{14}$ $\overline{3}$ $\overline{21}$ $\overline{5}$ $\overline{9}$. $\overline{17}$ $\overline{3}$ $\overline{7}$

$\overline{15}$ $\overline{3}$ $\overline{14}$ $\overline{9}'$ $\overline{14}$ $\overline{4}$ $\overline{4}$ $\overline{15}$ $\overline{5}$ $\overline{9}$. $\overline{17}$ $\overline{3}$ $\overline{7}$

$\overline{3}$ $\overline{14}$ $\overline{10}$ $\overline{17}$ $\overline{14}$ $\overline{4}$ $\overline{4}$ $\overline{15}$ $\overline{6}$ $\overline{4}$. $\overline{11}$ $\overline{3}'$

$\overline{15}$ $\overline{3}$ $\overline{17}$ $\overline{3}$ $\overline{7}$ $\overline{21}$ $\overline{8}$ $\overline{14}$ $\overline{9}$ $\overline{9}$ $\overline{3}$ $\overline{18}$ $\overline{4}$

$\overline{25}$ $\overline{4}$ $\overline{8}$ $\overline{10}$ $\overline{4}$ $\overline{15}$ $\overline{?}$ $\overline{10}$ $\overline{4}$ $\overline{9}'$ $\overline{11}$ $\overline{2}$ $\overline{3}$.

$\overline{13}$ $\overline{5}$ $\overline{12}$ $\overline{16}$ $\overline{7}$ $\overline{13}$ $\overline{17}$ $\overline{3}$ $\overline{7}$ $\overline{1}$ $\overline{6}$ $\overline{8}$ $\overline{9}$

$\overline{8}$ $\overline{14}$ $\overline{15}$ $\overline{21}$ $\overline{8}$ $\overline{10}$ $\overline{16}$.

Read John 5:1-15.

91

Answer on page 156

MAZE

Help Simon Z. (Zee) find the Zealot leader, Menachem, in the catacombs. For this maze, you will need to walk **on the lines**. Start and end with the blue circles.

Answer on page 156

Practice the next three letters of the Hebrew alphabet!

AYIN

This Hebrew letter is silent.

עַ

PE

This letter sounds like the **p** in pot.

פ

TSADI

This letter sounds like the **ts** in eats.

צַ

WORD CHANGE

Change the word TENT into CAMP one letter at a time.
Use the clues to help you figure out each word.

T E N T

— — — —   past tense of "to go"

— — — —   wish for

— — — —   rough bump on skin

— — — —   basket with wheels

— — — —   type of fish

C A M P

Answer on page 157

Word Search

ALTAR OF INCENSE

BEAUTIFUL GATE

CHAMBER OF LEPERS

CHAMBER OF OILS

CHAMBER OF NAZARITES

CHAMBER OF WOOD

COURT OF THE GENTILES

COURT OF THE WOMEN

FIRSTBORN GATE

FLAME GATE

HOLY OF HOLIES

HOLY PLACE

INNER COURT

JERUSALEM TEMPLE

LAMPSTAND

LIGHTING GATE

OUTER COURT

SACRIFICE GATE

SANCTUARY

SOLOMON'S PORCH

TABLE OF SHEWBREAD

VEIL

WATER GATE

Find the words describing parts of the Temple.

```
                    A C E C O I U R X U Q E O K A K E Q
                    O X A E E L P M E T M E L A S U R E J O
                    S E T I R A Z A N F O R E B M A H C P M
        M D A U           N D Q E           C L S U           G W C K
        L I E V           I M V S           F F C S           S O O K
        E D N Z           V B Y N           T L O O           R V U F
F S A N C T U A R Y T R U O C R E N N I B O P D A U L H O A F B K E A R F T M Z
E C A L P Y L O H T V R H Z L K C K J S D E J A M R O C H I B U F P B T B G E A
T Z K X C C A G T Y X Z U D I S N M M B S B E E E T M E N W Z Z L E V O E Y M F
V H T F O H M H E L K K K O G E I V Y N F Z A R G O O P K P A G Z L A F A A L C
        I U A V           O H I F           B A F N           F S T U
        R T M V           W T L O           W T T S           O A H T
        S E B Q           F I O R           E E H P           R C E I
        T R E O           O N H A           H D E O           E R G F
        B C R W           R G F T           S N W R           B I E U
        O O O A           E G O L           F A O C           M F N L
        R U F T           B A Y A           O T M H           A I T G
        N R O E           M T L K           E S E J           H C I A
        G T I R           A E O K           L P N G           C E L T
        A F L G           H A H P           B M S J           S G E E
        T K S A           C F L M           A A W C           B A S K
        E M K T           M Q C C           T L B R           Z T D X
        L M F E           K G S H           V N T A           T E Y E
```

WORD FIT

These people and places only fit into the puzzle one way. Use the number of letters in each word as a clue to where it could be put.

4 LETTERS
JOHN

MARY

5 LETTERS
HEROD

JACOB

JESUS

RAMAH

SIMON

6 LETTERS
ANDREW

HILLEL

JETHRO

PHILIP

SHIMON

THOMAS

7 LETTERS
JERICHO

MATTHEW

SHAMMAI

8 LETTERS
BIG JAMES

HERODIAS

THADDEUS

9 LETTERS
NATHANAEL

PHASAELIS

11 LETTERS
JORDAN RIVER

LITTLE JAMES

13 LETTERS
MARY MAGDALENE

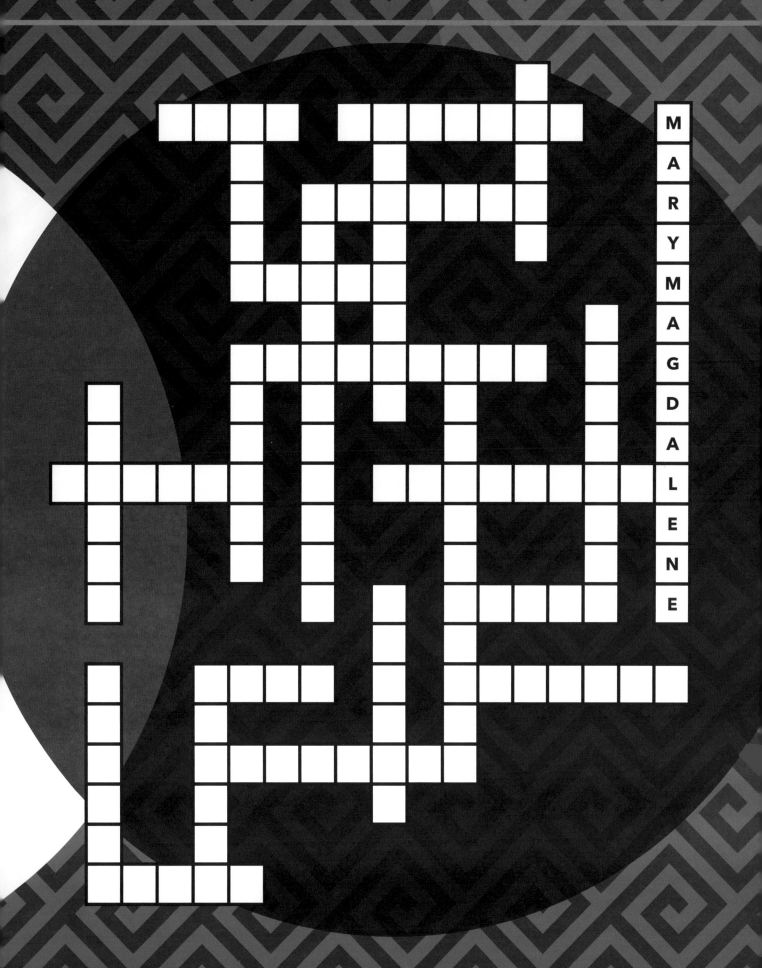

Answer on page 157

Which Fish?

Each colored fish in the puzzle represents a letter (all five vowels and two consonants). Figure out which fish carries which letter, and then read what Jesus said to John the Baptist.

🐟'M H🐟R🐟 F🐟R B🐟GG🐟R

P🐟RP🐟🐟🐟 🐟H🐟N 🐟H🐟

BR🐟🐟K🐟NG 🐟F R🐟L🐟🐟.

🐟'M G🐟🐟NG 🐟🐟 🐟🐟LL

🐟🐟🐟R🐟🐟 🐟H🐟🐟 M🐟K🐟

🐟N🐟🐟 🐟🐟🐟M🐟 P🐟🐟PL🐟

🐟ND N🐟🐟 🐟🐟 🐟🐟H🐟R🐟,

🐟ND 🐟H🐟🐟' J🐟🐟🐟 H🐟W

🐟🐟' G🐟🐟NG 🐟🐟 B🐟.

🐟'M 🐟LW🐟Y🐟 R🐟🐟DY 🐟🐟

D🐟 MY F🐟🐟H🐟R'🐟 W🐟LL ...

🐟H🐟🐟 D🐟🐟🐟N'🐟 M🐟K🐟 🐟🐟🐟

🐟🐟🐟Y.

Answer on page 157

SECRET DECODER

Use the code to read a statement someone spoke to Jesus. Use the numbers under the letters to solve the second coded message and discover who said it.

♆	♫	☼	⬤	✳	⚔	≋	✖	◎	✳	❖	✿	☾
A	B	C	D	E	F	G	H	I	J	K	L	M

⚙	⚑	🐈	◆	★	💰	✡	✝	🗝	🕊	●	◻	✦
N	O	P	Q	R	S	T	U	V	W	X	Y	Z

Who said this to Jesus?

‾‾ ‾‾ ‾‾ ‾‾   ‾‾ ‾‾ ‾‾
1   2   3   4   5   6   7

‾‾ ‾‾ ‾‾ ‾‾ ‾‾ ‾‾ ‾‾
8   9 10 11 12 13 14

Answer on page 157

NUMBER CODE

Use the grid to figure out which letters go where, so you can read what Jesus said to Zee about his calling. We have given you some numbers to begin.

A	B	C	D	E	F	G	H	I	J	K	L	M
2							16	1	18			10

N	O	P	Q	R	S	T	U	V	W	X	Y	Z
6		15	24		3			19		26	9	17

9　8　22　　2　12　4　　6　8　7　　2　5　8　6　4

1　6　　10　1　3　22　6　23　4　12　3　7　2　6　23　1　6　13.

14　22　7　　6　8　7　　7　8　　25　8　12　12　9.

1　　10　　15　12　4　15　2　12　1　6　13　　3　8　10　4

7　16　1　6　13　　7　8　　3　16　2　12　4　　25　1　7　16

7　16　4　　25　8　12　5　23.　　20　8　12　　6　8　25,

25　2　6　7　1　6　13　　9　8　22　　14　9　　10　9

3　1　23　4　　16　2　3　　7　8　　14　4

4　6　8　22　13　16.　　6　8　　8　6　4　　14　22　9　3

7　16　4　1　12　　25　2　9　　1　6　7　8　　8　22　12

13　12　8　22　15　　14　4　11　2　22　3　4　　8　20

3　15　4　11　1　2　5　　3　21　1　5　5　3.

Answer on page 157

LETTER PAIRS

The letters in the message from Jesus to John the Baptist have gotten mixed up! Use the grid to figure out which letters switched places. Put the right letter back on the line so you can read the message.

Some of the letter pairs are already listed to help you get started.

A	B	C	D	E	F	G	H	I	J	K	L	M
I		S				W	L	A	V	X	H	
N	O	P	Q	R	S	T	U	V	W	X	Y	Z
	Z		C				J	G	K			Q

'
‾ ‾ ‾ ‾‾‾ ‾‾‾‾‾
A T FEM GIDFAFW

‾‾‾; ‾‾‾ '‾‾
UEY UEY DO

‾‾‾‾‾ ‾‾‾‾
REAFW GLIM

'
‾‾‾ ‾‾ ‾‾‾‾‾‾‾
UEY DO CYBBECOR

‾‾ ‾‾. '‾ ‾‾‾
ME RE A T EFHU

‾‾‾‾‾‾‾‾‾ ‾‾‾
DOTAFRAFW UEY

‾‾ ‾‾ ‾‾‾‾ ‾‾
ME PO CYDO ME

'
‾‾‾‾‾‾ ‾‾ ‾‾‾ ‾
HACMOF ME WER C

‾‾‾‾‾ ‾‾ ‾‾‾ ‾‾
JEASO IC UEY RE

‾‾.
AM

Answer on page 157

A VARIETY OF VESSELS

USE THE LETTERS AND NUMBERS TO SHOW WHERE EACH OF THESE PIECES BELONG IN THE PUZZLE. WE GOT YOU STARTED! ⟶ B1 _____

_____

_____

_____

_____

_____

_____

_____

Answer on page 158

LEMON LETTERS

Each of the lemon trees have enough lemons to spell one word. Match the lemon trees with the baskets to figure out which set of letters belongs where. Then, unscramble the letters and write the word in the spaces under each basket. When you are done, you will be able to read what Mary prayed as she collected lemons from the trees in the grove.

_ _ _ _ _ _ _ ARE YOU, _ _ _ _ OUR GOD,

_ _ _ _ OF THE _ _ _ _ _ _ _ _ WHOSE _ _ _ _ _

LACKS _ _ _ _ _ _ _ _ , AND WHO _ _ _ _ WONDROUS

_ _ _ _ _ _ _ _ _ _ AND GOOD _ _ _ _ _ , THROUGH

WHICH HE _ _ _ _ _ _ PLEASURE TO THE _ _ _ _ _ _ _ _ ,

OF _ _ _ _ .

Practice the next two letters of the Hebrew alphabet!

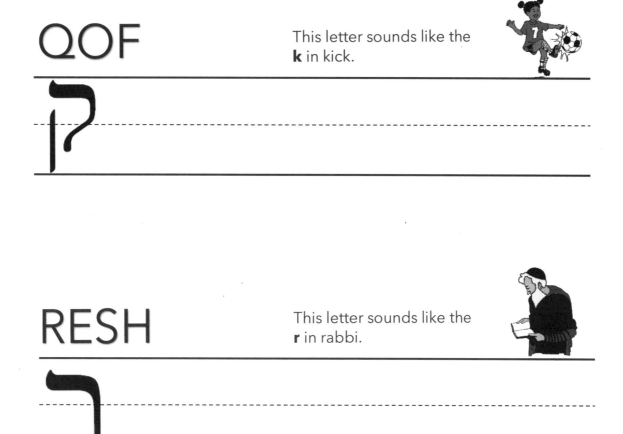

QOF

ק

This letter sounds like the **k** in kick.

RESH

ר

This letter sounds like the **r** in rabbi.

Word Search

Find more characters and places in the word search!

AARON

ABIATHAR

AHIMALECH

DAVID

DIONYSUS

DUNASH

ELAM

GAVIUS

HOHJ

JERICHO

LAMECH

MADAI

MICAH

NOB

SAUL

SHOOB

WADI KELT

YAFA

YUSSEF

```
B H G Q       M P K T
Y O P F H   O M A S T
S E  H O S T   H T I D   X L
A E D I A H R   P Y N C A H G
U L J N S U S Y N O I D A I Q
L K U Q N C H C E L A M I H A
  D A F A Y U S S E F I X B
    G A V I U S R
  J E R I C H O N D D R V D
K E Q Q W A D I K E L T X I J
N L I N A B I A T H A R R V F
W A B O S U B   B H M B L A I
B M  R V J K   K O E O   D Z
  M A Z N A   G H C N K
  D A R U     J H X Q
```

WORD FIT

Jesus and His disciples sometimes didn't have a lot to eat. Mother Mary and Ramah have ventured out to find flowers that can be eaten. Figure out how to fit these flowers in the puzzle. The words only fit one way. Use the number of letters in each word as a clue to where it could be put.

4 LETTERS
ROSE

5 LETTERS
LILAC
PANSY
PEONY
POPPY
VIOLA

6 LETTERS
ALLIUM
DAHLIA
VIOLET

7 LETTERS
BEGONIA
DAY LILY
FUCHSIA
JASMINE

8 LETTERS
CAMELLIA
HIBISCUS
LAVENDER
MAGNOLIA
MARIGOLD

9 LETTERS
CARNATION
DANDELION

10 LETTERS
NASTURTIUM
SNAP DRAGON

12 LETTERS
APPLE BLOSSOM
CHIVE BLOSSOM

13 LETTERS
CHERRY BLOSSOM
CHRYSANTHEMUM
SQUASH BLOSSOM

C H E R R Y B L O S S O M

Answer on page 158

Which Fish?

Each colored fish in the puzzle represents a letter (all five vowels and two consonants). Figure out which fish carries which letter, and then read the words Jesus spoke to the religious leaders.

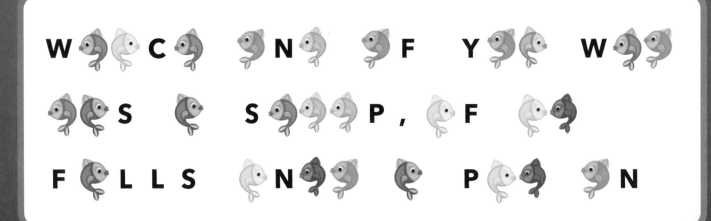

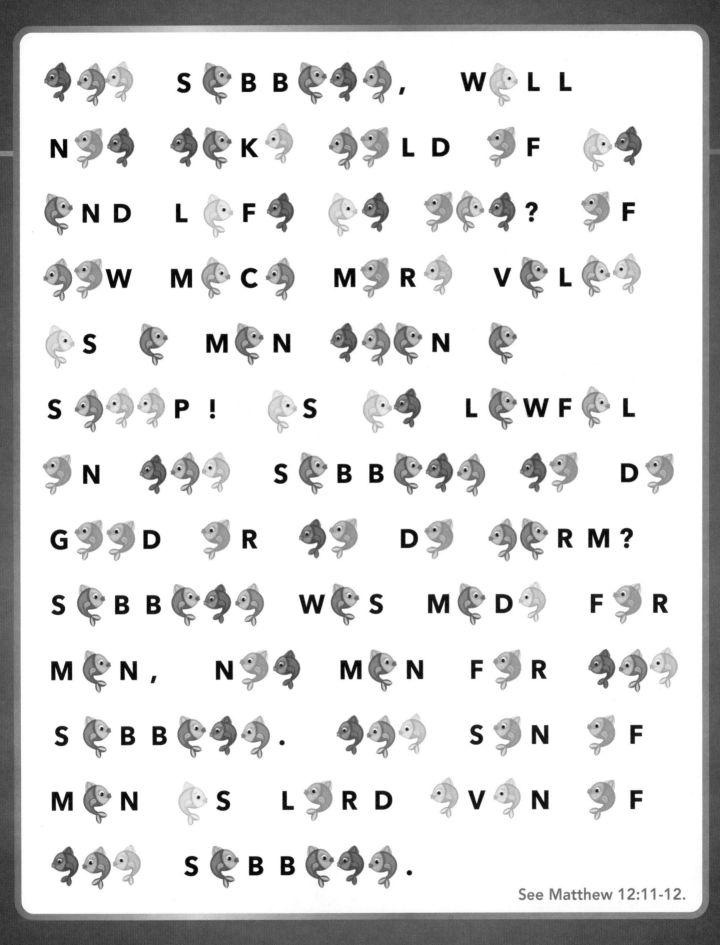

See Matthew 12:11-12.

Answer on page 158

NUMBER CODE

Use the grid to figure out which letters go where, so you can read what Jesus said to one of His followers when they returned to camp. We have given you some numbers to begin.

Unscramble the letters in the highlighted boxes to find out who Jesus was talking to.

A	B	C	D	E	F	G	H	I	J	K	L	M
	19		1			8						

N	O	P	Q	R	S	T	U	V	W	X	Y	Z
6		12	25		7				24		26	

10   22 20 2 7   17 5 6 7   [14] 9 20 3

8 1 5 3 7 .   7 8 1   15 5 7 8 1 3

22 20 2 7   17 5 6 7 2   14 9 20 3

8 1 [5] 3 7 .   21 10 23 1   20 2   7 8 5 7 '

17 8 10 13 8   14 9 20   8 5 23 1 '   5 6 16

7 8 1   3 1 2 7   17 10 4 4   13 9 11 1

10 6   7 10 [11] 1 .   16 10 16   14 9 20

3 1 5 4 4 14   7 8 10 6 18   14 9 20   16

6 1 23 1 [3]   2 7 3 20 21 21 4 1   9 3

2 10 6   5 21 5 10 6 ?

Who was Jesus talking to?

MAZE

Exit the campground and collect as many lentils as you can while you make your way back to camp without crossing the same path twice.

How many lentils did you collect? _____

LETTER WHEEL

Use the letters in the wheel to fill in the blank letters and complete Matthew's question to Simon. Letters can be used multiple times.

_H_ _ _F Y_U _ _ _ _

CU_ _FF F_ _M

J_SUS BY S_M_ _H_NG

_N Y_U_ P_S_?

_ _ULDN'_ Y_U _ _N_

H_LP G_ _ _ _NG B_CK

_ _ H_M _S S_ _N

_S P_SS_BL_?

Answer on page 158

WORD (IN) WORD

Use the definitions to figure out the small words. The letters with arrows "drop" down into the boxes below them to help you complete the bigger words, which will spell out the **tribes of Israel**. Use the words below to figure out the tribes but be careful; some are not right!

BENJAMIN	LEVI	NAPHTALI
REUBEN	MANASSEH	DAN
JACOB	JUDAH	JOEL
JOSEPH	ZEBULUN	GAD
DANIEL	ISSACHAR	ISAIAH
SIMEON	EPHRAIM	ASHER

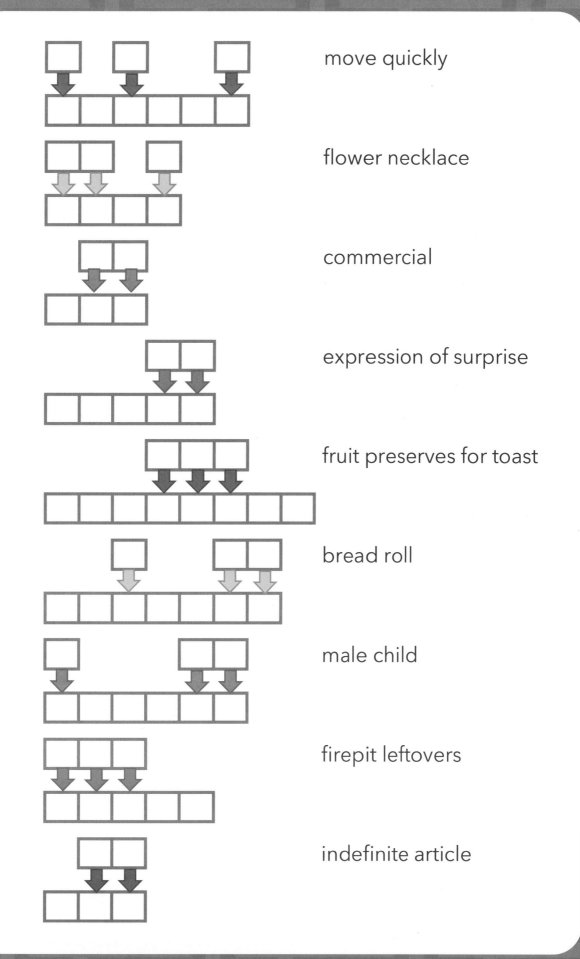

move quickly

flower necklace

commercial

expression of surprise

fruit preserves for toast

bread roll

male child

firepit leftovers

indefinite article

Answer on page 159

TANGLE OF TWIGS

USE THE LETTERS AND NUMBERS
TO SHOW WHERE EACH OF THESE
PIECES BELONG IN THE PUZZLE.
WE GOT YOU STARTED! ———————→ F7

F7

_____

_____

_____

_____

_____

_____

_____

_____

_____

Alphabet practice!

Practice the next two letters of the Hebrew alphabet!

SHIN

This letter sounds like the **sh** in ship.

TAW

This letter sounds like the **t** in teach.

WORD CHANGE

Change the word JAIL into FREE one letter at a time.
Use the clues to help you figure out each word.

J A I L

— — — — what wags on a dog

— — — — not short

— — — — shopping place

— — — — thick shake

— — — — from solid to liquid

— — — — be introduced to

— — — — plural of foot

— — — — worry

F R E E

  Answer on page 159

SECRET DECODER

Use the code to read what Jesus told
Philip about the sermon He was preparing.
Use the numbers under the letters to solve
the second question.

A	B	C	D	E	F	G	H	I	J	K	L	M

N	O	P	Q	R	S	T	U	V	W	X	Y	Z

What was Jesus giving the people?

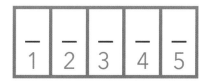

Answer on page 159

Logic Grid

Some of the disciples are having a rock-throwing contest to decide what tasks they will be assigned to. Use the clues below to figure out who won the rock-throwing competition and what type of rocks were thrown by whom.

The grid will help you make sense of the jumbled information.

CLUES

- Simon and Andrew's rocks are obsidian and limestone, not necessarily in that order.
- The person throwing the piece of slate finished first.
- John came in last place.
- Andrew didn't finish in second place.
- The person who threw obsidian didn't come in third place.

		POSITION				STONE			
		FIRST	SECOND	THIRD	FOURTH	OBSIDIAN	MARBLE	SLATE	LIMESTONE
DISCIPLE	SIMON								
	BIG JAMES								
	ANDREW								
	JOHN								
STONE	OBSIDIAN								
	MARBLE								
	SLATE								
	LIMESTONE								

Answer on page 159

MYSTERY LETTERS

Using the color code, fill in the missing letters to see what Jesus said to some of the disciples. There are two mystery letters you will need to figure out to complete the message.

					?	?
A	E	I	O	U		

"Get used to different." SIMON

Y _ _ _ L L _ R _ _ _ _ N

_ _ H V _ _ _ L _ R N

H W _ _ D _ H S

R _ _ _ R D L _ S S _ F

W H _ _ ' S H _ P P _ N _ N , _ _ _ D _ R B _ D . _ _ H S

_ S _ N L Y _ _ _ N _ _ _

_ _ _ M R _ D _ F F _ C _ L

Y _ _ C _ N ' _ J _ S

S H _ _ D _ W N W H _ N Y _ _

_ R _ F _ _ R F _ L . W H _ _

_ R _ Y _ _ _ _ N _ _ _

D _ W H _ N _ ' M _ N

L _ N _ R H _ R ?

Answer on page 159

LETTER PAIRS

The letters in the Scripture that Mary is teaching Ramah have gotten mixed up! Use the grid to figure out which letters switched places. Put the right letter back on the line so you can read the message.

Some of the letter pairs are already listed to help you get started.

A	B	C	D	E	F	G	H	I	J	K	L	M
R		K		S					X	D		

N	O	P	Q	R	S	T	U	V	W	X	Y	Z
Y		Z	B	F						J	O	Q

__ __ ____ ___ ___
P O S B E P A V E F G Y L

_____ ____ ___
C U K K A G S B Y P O Y I

____ _ ___ _____
V C A G U V E F R A U G N

____ __ _____'
P E K A U G F A H B A L'

_____ ____
U G L B U H E L A T O V Y W A G

__ ___ _____ __
U G L C A K A M L C F Y S

___ ____ . ____
L C A A E B L C O Y I B

____ ___ __
A O A F F E V P O

_____
I G S Y B P A K

_____ . __
F.I R F L E G H A U G

____ ____ ____
O Y I B R Y Y D V A B A

_____ ____ ___
V B U L L A G A W A B O Y G A

__ ___ ____ ____
Y S L C A K E O F L C E L

____ _____ ___
V A B A S Y B P A K S Y B

__ .
P A

See Psalm 39:15-16.

139   Answer on page 160

CROSSWORD FUN

Jesus did things that upset the religious leaders. Use the clues to solve the crossword showing what Jesus was accused of. The answers are scrambled in the box below.

- Uses a _ _ _ _ _ _ title for himself from the prophet Daniel:
     1 DOWN

   _ _ _   _ _   _ _ _.
     8 DOWN

- Claims _ _ _ _ _ _ _ _ _ _ to forgive _ _ _ _.
     3 DOWN   2 ACROSS

- Violates _ _ _ _ _ _ _ _ multiple times
     5 DOWN

   and commands _ _ _ _ _ _ to do the same.
     10 ACROSS

- Eats with _ _ _   _ _ _ _ _ _ _ _ _ _ _ and _ _ _ _ _ _ _ _.
     9 ACROSS   4 ACROSS

- Has _ _ _ _ _ _ _ _ _ _ who are _ _ _ _ _.
     7 ACROSS   11 ACROSS

- Hangs out with _ _ _ _ _ _ _ _ _ and _ _ _ _ _ _ _.
     12 ACROSS   6 DOWN

VIDNEI	XAT LEOCLORTSC
THABSAB	INSS
EOZALTS	WRFLSOOLE
RSEINSN	NOS FO NAM
RSEOTH	NSEGILTE
HRYAUTIOT	NEWOM

"I'm here to make things better, not worse." JESUS

Answer on page 160

PURPLE PETALS

USE THE LETTERS AND NUMBERS
TO SHOW WHERE EACH OF THESE
PIECES BELONG IN THE PUZZLE.
WE GOT YOU STARTED! ⟶ <u>E8</u>

Answer on page 160

A B C D E F

1
2
3
4
5
6
7
8

143

Logic Grid

Some of the women wanted Jesus to add a sash to His usual clothing to make Him stand out during the Sermon on the Mount. Each woman provided a different color sash with unique meanings. See if you can figure out which woman had what color sash, what the color was a symbol of, and in what order it was tried on.

The grid will help you make sense of the jumbled information.

CLUES

- MOTHER MARY's color was tried on fourth. RAMAH's color didn't get tried on first.
- Of the first and third sashes, one of them was PURPLE, the other represented PEACE.
- Three of the women are: TAMAR, the woman whose sash was PURPLE, and the woman whose color represented LIGHT.
- TAMAR's sash wasn't BLUE. She didn't have the sash that stood for PEACE or ROYALTY.
- MOTHER MARY's sash either meant LIGHT, or it was BLUE.
- RAMAH's sash was PURPLE.
- LOVE is either represented by RED or it was MARY MAGDALENE's choice.

		COLOR				ORDER				MEANING			
		BLUE	GOLD	PURPLE	RED	FIRST	SECOND	THIRD	FOURTH	LIGHT	LOVE	PEACE	ROYALTY
WOMAN	MOTHER MARY												
	RAMAH												
	MARY MAGDALENE												
	TAMAR												
MEANING	LIGHT												
	LOVE												
	PEACE												
	ROYALTY												
ORDER	FIRST												
	SECOND												
	THIRD												
	FOURTH												

MATCH UP

The Beatitudes were part of the Sermon on the Mount that Jesus preached to a very large crowd. He spoke of the qualities and their blessings as being a map for those who wanted to find Him.

Match the quality with the blessing, and then see if you can remember who Jesus pictured as He spoke each one. In the little boxes with the blessing, write the number that matches the quality. In the little boxes with the people, write the number showing who Jesus was thinking of.

BLESSED ARE...

| 1 the poor in spirit… | 2 those who mourn… | 3 the meek… | 4 those who hunger and thirst for righteousness |
| 5 the merciful… | 6 the pure in heart… | 7 the peacemakers… | 8 those who are persecuted for righteousness' sake… |

| ☐ …for they shall receive mercy. | ☐ … for theirs is the kingdom of heaven. | ☐ … for they shall inherit the earth. | ☐ … for they shall be called sons of God. |
| ☐ … for they shall be satisfied. | ☐ …for theirs is the kingdom of heaven. | ☐ …for they shall see God. | ☐ …for they shall be comforted. |

| ☐ Mother Mary | ☐ Nathanael | ☐ Little James & Thaddeus | ☐ Big James & John |
| ☐ John the Baptist & Matthew | ☐ Mary, Ramah, and Thomas | ☐ Andrew | ☐ Philip, Simon, and Zee |

Answer on page 160

MAZE

Help Little James, Thaddeus, and Nathanael find the spot for the Sermon on the Mount.

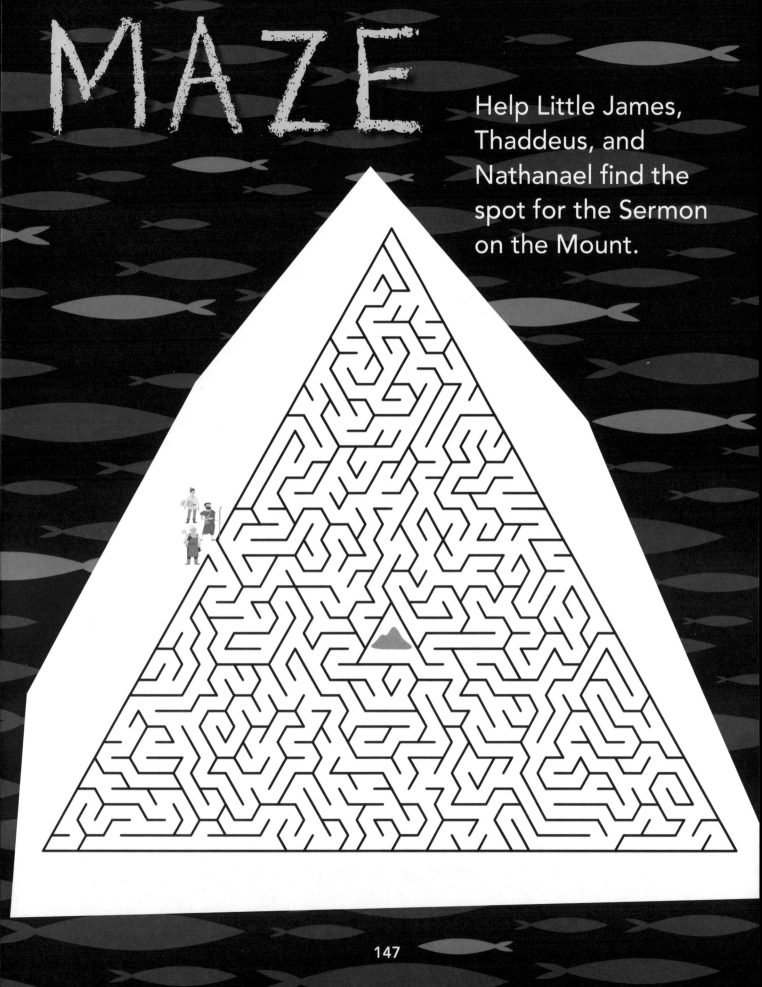

Word Search

Look at all the people who showed up for the Sermon on the Mount!

ANDREW

ATTICUS

BARNABY

BIG JAMES

DASHA

EDEN

GAIUS

GAMALIEL

HUSHAM

JESUS

JOHN

JUDAS

LITTLE JAMES

MARY MAGDALENE

MATTHEW

MOTHER MARY

NATHANAEL

PHILIP

RAMAH

SALOME

SHULA

SIMON

TAMAR

THADDEUS

THOMAS

YUSSIF

ZEBEDEE

ZEE

```
                        Z  W
                        E  R
                        B  U
                        E  Z
P  N                                                                    I
   T  O              G  U  D  G  Z  B                              X  N
      Q  M        W  E  A  H  E  X  S  U  S  E  J              A  E
         B  I  S  G  N  F  Z  G  E  M  A  H  S  U  H  T      J  D
         G  S  U  L  E  A  N  A  H  T  A  N  T  A  S  L  E
      S  A  X  W  K  O  V  V  T  D  C  E  K  M  X  L  H
         I  P  W  A  M  A  R  Y  M  A  G  D  A  L  E  N  E  C
      G  J  T  H  O  M  A  S  Q  Z  S  V  R  D  U  O  T  Z  A
      P  S  U  S  S  Q  N  B  F  I  S  S  U  Y  L  G  W  E  Y  Y
      G  P  Z  D  D  S  E  M  A  J  E  L  T  T  I  L  R  E  O  E
T  L  L  F  H  H  L  L  A  R  O  M  T  Y  K  T  I  W  E  H  T  T  A  M  L  E  D  X
X  B  K  F  C  I  X  Q  S  S  R  D  J  N  W  Z  I  A  R  I  H  N  Y  N  M  K  Y  R
      B  L  A  O  R  U  A  Y  S  K  G  A  M  A  L  I  E  L  N  O
      V  I  L  N  Z  H  R  J  N  U  S  E  M  A  J  G  I  B  L  M
      R  P  U  B  I  A  O  H  N  W  C  U  C  B  D  I  O  A  W
      G  H  S  M  M  O  U  E  B  B  I  C  N  Q  A  S  F  H
      R  S  R  U  J  U  R  X  A  F  G  T  Y  K  T  S  A
      M  E  M  M  I  D  C  M  R  S  G  W  T  W  J  M  H
   K  H        T  K  N  A  R  J  N  U  L  Y  C  A  A        F  A
   Y  T              A  Q  U  G  B  A  E  M  A  W  R              Y  G
H  O                    J  C  B  D  Z  A                          U  K
M                          Y  D                                  X  Y
                           O  A
                           Q  H
                           Q  T
```

ANSWER KEY

PAGE 4

B8   **E2**   **B6**

F6   **D7**   **E5**

C1   **D4**   **B3**

PAGE 7

If you tried to write every single thing He did; the world itself could not contain the books that would be written.

PAGE 8

Across: 3. Thaddeus
6. Andrew 7. Thomas
8. Mary Magdalene
11. Simon
Down: 1. Matthew
2. Nathanael 4. Philip
5. James 9. Mary
10. John

PAGE 15

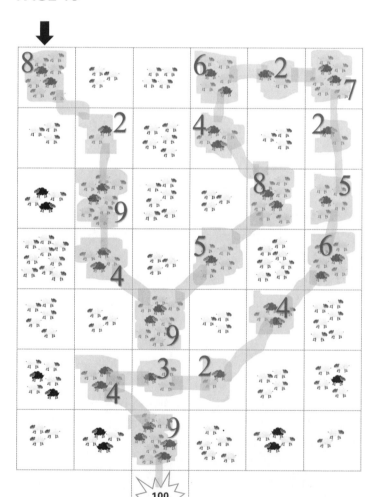

PAGE 15

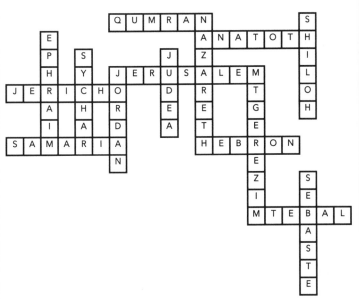

PAGES 18-19

A	B	C	D	E	F	G	H	I	J	K	L	M
6	11	22	17	3	26	13	19	8	15	20	2	9

N	O	P	Q	R	S	T	U	V	W	X	Y	Z
4	18	7	25	12	1	5	14	24	21	16	10	23

There will be more joy in heaven over one sinner who repents than over ninety-nine righteous who need no repentance.

PAGE 17

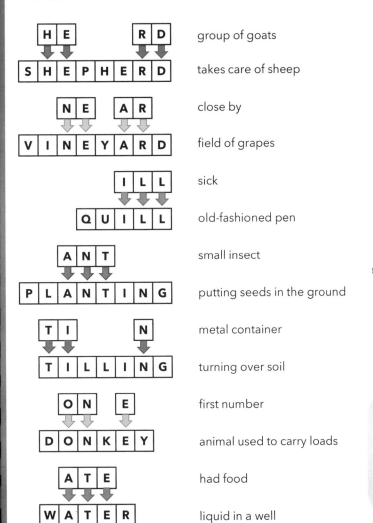

HE RD	group of goats	
SHEPHERD	takes care of sheep	
NE AR	close by	
VINEYARD	field of grapes	
ILL	sick	
QUILL	old-fashioned pen	
ANT	small insect	
PLANTING	putting seeds in the ground	
TI N	metal container	
TILLING	turning over soil	
ON E	first number	
DONKEY	animal used to carry loads	
ATE	had food	
WATER	liquid in a well	

PAGE 21

Heaven and earth will pass away, but my words will never pass away.

PAGES 22, 23

In the beginning, God created the heavens and the earth.
The earth was without form and void, and darkness was over the face of the deep.

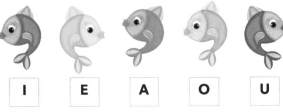

I	E	A	O	U

PAGE 24

Mary = cloves; John = garlic;
Matthew = onion; Simon = pepper;
Andrew = salt

PAGE 26

SEED, WEED, WELD, WELT, MELT, MALT, MALE, MILE, TILE, TILL

PAGE 28

D3	A4	E7
D8	B7	E4
C5	E1	B2

PAGES 34-35

A	B	C	D	E	F	G	H	I	J	K	L	M
5	19	8	1	15	23	10	4	24	17	21	11	14

N	O	P	Q	R	S	T	U	V	W	X	Y	Z
9	6	20	13	2	16	7	22	26	3	18	12	25

If this Rabbi Jesus from Nazareth called you, it means you already have everything you need for right now, and He will give you the rest in time. What you think you know doesn't matter, only that Jesus chose you. That's where your confidence comes from now.

PAGE 31

PAGES 32-33

I was something else once too. Once you've met the Messiah, am is all that matters. People out there want to define us by our pasts, but we do things differently because of Him. Mystery letters – blue = L; gray = M

PAGES 36-37

Hear my prayer O Lord; let my cry come to you. Do not hide your face from me in the day of my distress. Incline your ear to me; answer me speedily in the day when I call.

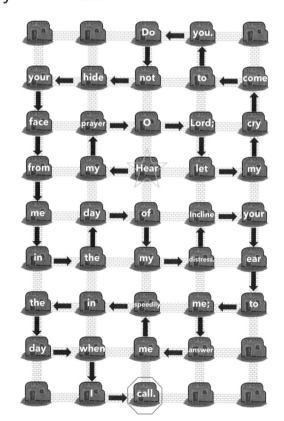

PAGES 38-39

I am thankful before you, living and enduring King, for you have mercifully restored my soul within me. Great is your faithfulness.

O	M	A	U	I	N	E

PAGES 40-41

Every one of those people I called for a reason. They each bring something unique and important to the whole. I want every voice heard and none silenced. Everyone can learn from each other.

Jesus said this to Simon.

PAGE 42

PLAN, CLAN, CLAP, FLAP, FLAT, FEAT, FEST, FAST, PAST, POST, POSE, HOSE, HOME

PAGE 44

B1   F4   F2

B4   C6   A6

E6   D3   B8

PAGE 46

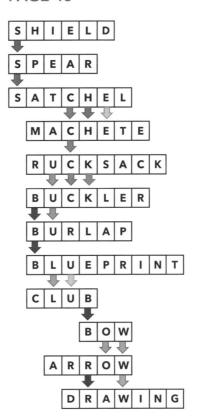

PAGE 47

If we do not make time for friends, we will not have any.

PAGE 51

Don't look at him; look at me. When you were in your lowest moment, and you were alone, I did not turn my face from you. I saw you.

PAGE 53

1) Thirteen; 2) Fig tree;
3) Philip; 4) Ramah;
5) Nathanael;
6) Nazareth; 7)Matthew;
8) Big James; 9) Andrew;
10) Torah

PAGE 55

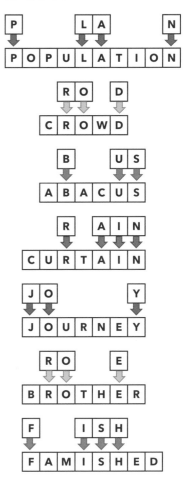

PAGE 57

Big James wore a brown tunic and pulled the cart at 10:00.

Andrew wore a yellow tunic and pulled the cart at 2:00.

Simon wore a green tunic and pulled the cart at 12:00.

John wore a blue tunic and pulled the cart at 8:00.

PAGE 59

SINS, TINS, TONS, TOPS, HOPS, HOPE, HOLE, HOLY

PAGE 60

A + F
B + N
G + S
D + M
K + R

C + O
E + P
Q + I
J + T
H + L

PAGES 62-63

No amount of learning can get you closer to God or make you more or less precious to Him. He's always right here, right now, with you, and for you. Mystery letters – yellow = N; gray = T

PAGE 65

If I ascend to heaven, you are there. If I make my bed in the depths, you are there.

PAGES 66-67

A	B	C	D	E	F	G	H	I	J	K	L	M
12	21	5	18	2	22	16	9	11	3	14	25	7

N	O	P	Q	R	S	T	U	V	W	X	Y	Z
13	20	8	24	4	10	23	26	1	15	6	17	19

I don't think He's waiting for us to be holy. I think He's here because we can't be holy without Him.

PAGE 68

Said he wouldn't mind being famous — ANDREW
Took and ate pork once — MATTHEW
Stayed in the tent healing all day — LITTLE JAMES
Said she always did what she was told — JOHN
Could recite half the Torah and loved the rules — SIMON
Had a form of paralysis — RAMAH
Ate meat with cheese once — BIG JAMES
Left everything when she lost a parent — MOTHER MARY
Washed Jesus' feet after a long day of ministry — THADDEUS
Said he would never forgive Matthew for his betrayal — THOMAS
A rule-follower from birth — MARY MAGDALENE
Had a lot of money before following Jesus — JESUS

PAGE 71

Blessed are you, Lord our God, King of the Universe, who brings sleep to my eyes

PAGES 73-74

To suffer for centuries and centuries because of it, but to still commit to it, to protect our heritage even though it never stops being painful, because the one comfort we have is to know that we're doing it together. That we're all suffering together. But if we just wait a little longer, if we hold tight just a little more, we'll have rescue. Because we're chosen. All of us.

Simon was talking about *being Jewish*.

PAGE 76

C4   E7   D6

E2   B7   B3

A6   B1   F4

PAGE 79

Crossword answers:
- UPPER CITY
- AGORA GATE
- SOLOMONS PORCH
- POOL OF BETHESDA
- ANTONIA FORTRESS
- SUKKAH
- WILDERNESS
- LOWER CITY
- DESERT PLATEAU
- HEBRON MARKET
- TEMPLE MOUNT
- ARCHWAY
- PRAETORIUM
- CACHALOT (ROYAL STOA)

PAGES 84-85

| U | I | T | E | O | S | A |

Fear not, O Zion; let not your hands grow weak. The Lord your God is in your midst, a mighty one who will save. He will rejoice over you with gladness; He will quiet you by His love; He will exult over you with loud singing. Behold at that time, I will deal with all your oppressors. And I will save the lame and gather the outcast, and I will change their shame into praise and renown in all the earth.

PAGES 86-87

BIG JAMES' QUESTION: Everyone who survives of all the nations that have attacked Jerusalem shall go up year after year to worship the King, the Lord of hosts, and to celebrate the Feast of Tabernacles. Our enemies will celebrate with us? How do they understand?

JESUS' ANSWER: Everyone has wandered in the wilderness at some point.

PAGE 83

- S — SOLDIER
- G — BODYGUARD
- P — TRAINEE
- O — CENTURION
- K — VENDOR
- H — CITIZEN
- L — ONLOOKER
- C — TRAVELER
- J — RABBI
- A — HIGH PRIEST
- I — ZEALOT
- F — RECRUIT
- B — SERVANT
- N — FARMER
- R — CRIMINAL
- E — HERDER
- T — MAGISTRATE
- D — DISCIPLE
- Q — LABORER
- M — CUSTOMER

PAGE 88

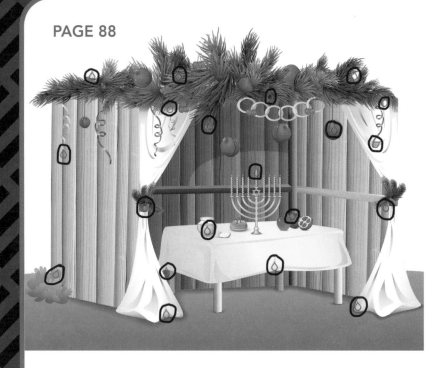

PAGES 90-91

A	B	C	D	E	F	G	H	I	J	K	L	M
8	18	12	15	4	20	2	25	5	23	16	10	6

N	O	P	Q	R	S	T	U	V	W	X	Y	Z
14	3	13	19	1	11	9	7	24	21	26	17	22

I'm not asking about who's helping or not helping, who's in your way… I'm asking about you. You don't want false hope again, I understand. But this pool has nothing for you; it means nothing, and you know it. You don't need it. You only need me. So, do you want to be healed? Let's go. Pick up your mat and walk.

PAGE 89

God said to live in a booth for seven days during this feast, to commemorate how the children of Israel lived in temporary shelters for forty years in the desert.

The Feast of Tabernacles was one of three pilgrimage holidays when every able-bodied Israelite man must travel to Jerusalem and present himself before Adonai.

PAGE 93

PAGE 95

TENT, WENT, WANT, WART, CART, CARP, CAMP

PAGE 99

PAGES 100-101

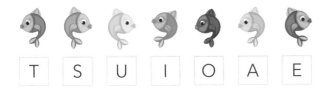

| T | S | U | I | O | A | E |

I'm here for bigger purposes than the breaking of rules. I'm going to tell stories that make sense to some people and not to others, and that's just how it's going to be. I'm always ready to do my Father's will… that doesn't make it easy.

PAGES 102-103

You know that my heart is yours; my life is yours, and the sole reason I was miraculously conceived by two old people was so I could prepare the way for you. I'm just impatient for you to get to work.

John the Baptist said this to Jesus.

PAGES 104-105

A	B	C	D	E	F	G	H	I	J	K	L	M
2	14	11	23	4	20	13	16	1	18	21	5	10

N	O	P	Q	R	S	T	U	V	W	X	Y	Z
6	8	15	24	12	3	7	22	19	25	26	9	17

You are not alone in misunderstanding. But not to worry. I'm preparing something to share with the world. For now, wanting you by my side has to be enough. No one buys their way into our group because of special skills.

PAGES 106-107

A	B	C	D	E	F	G	H	I	J	K	L	M
I	P	S	R	O	N	W	L	A	V	X	H	T
N	O	P	Q	R	S	T	U	V	W	X	Y	Z
F	E	B	Z	D	C	M	Y	J	G	K	U	Q

I'm not warning you; you're doing what you're supposed to do.
I'm only reminding you to be sure to listen to God's voice as you do it.

PAGE 108

B6	E7	C4
D5	F3	E2
C3	B8	E4

PAGE 110

BLESSED are you LORD our God, KING of the UNIVERSE, whose WORLD lacks NOTHING, and who MADE wondrous CREATURES and good TREES, through which He BRINGS pleasure to the CHILDREN of ADAM.

PAGE 117

PAGES 118-119

H	U	I	O	T	E	A

Which one of you who has a sheep, if it falls into a pit on the Sabbath, will not take hold of it and lift it out? Of how much more value is a man than a sheep! Is it lawful on the Sabbath to do good or to do harm? Sabbath was made for man, not man for the Sabbath. The Son of Man is Lord even of the Sabbath.

PAGES 120-121

A	B	C	D	E	F	G	H	I	J	K	L	M
5	19	13	16	1	15	21	8	10	22	18	4	11

N	O	P	Q	R	S	T	U	V	W	X	Y	Z
6	9	12	25	3	2	7	20	23	17	24	14	26

I just want your heart. The Father just wants your heart. Give us that, which you have, and the rest will come in time. Did you really think you'd never struggle or sin again?

Jesus was talking to Mary.

PAGE 123

15 lentils.

PAGE 125

What if you were cut off from Jesus by something in your past? Wouldn't you want help getting back to Him as soon as possible?

PAGE 127

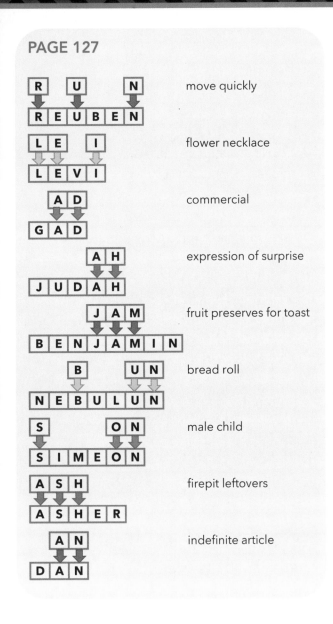

Puzzle	Clue
RUN → REUBEN	move quickly
LEI → LEVI	flower necklace
AD → GAD	commercial
AH → JUDAH	expression of surprise
JAM → BENJAMIN	fruit preserves for toast
BUN → NEBULUN	bread roll
SON → SIMEON	male child
ASH → ASHER	firepit leftovers
AN → DAN	indefinite article

PAGE 128

C5 B7 B2

C8 D6 D3

A4 E4 A5

PAGE 131

JAIL, TAIL, TALL, MALL, MALT, MELT, MEET, FEET, FRET, FREE

PAGES 132-133

This sermon will have thousands of people. I won't be directing it to one people group over another. But what I say will be for each and every one of them. They're coming because the word is spreading from the signs and wonders, but I'll be giving them something far more important.

What was Jesus giving them? Truth.

PAGE 135

Simon threw obsidian and came second. Big James threw slate and came first. Andrew threw limestone and came third. John threw marble and came last.

PAGES 136-137

You all are going to have to learn how to do this regardless of what's happening, good or bad. This is only going to get more difficult; you can't just shut down when you are fearful. What are you going to do when I'm no longer here? Prayer is the first step in getting your mind and heart right; it's why you see me go to it so often. Mystery letters – yellow = T; gray = G

PAGES 138-139

A	B	C	D	E	F	G	H	I	J	K	L	M
E	R	H	K	A	S	N	C	U	X	D	T	P
N	O	P	Q	R	S	T	U	V	W	X	Y	Z
G	Y	M	Z	B	F	L	I	W	V	J	O	Q

My frame was not hidden from you when I was being made in secret, intricately woven in the depths of the earth. Your eyes saw my unformed substance. In your book were written every one of the days that were formed for me.

PAGES 140-141

Across: 2. Sins 4. Sinners
7. Followers 9. Tax collectors
10. Others 11. Women
12. Gentiles
Down: 1. Divine 3. Authority
5. Shabbat 6. Zealots
8. Son of Man

PAGE 142

B3   B6   A5

E6   D4   E2

C7   B1   F6

PAGE 145

Mary Magdalene had a blue sash, symbolizing peace, and it was tried on first.

Tamar had a red sash, symbolizing love, and it was tried on second.

Ramah had a purple sash, symbolizing royalty, and it was tried on third.

Mother Mary had a gold sash, symbolizing light, and it was tried on last.

PAGE 146

5 ...for they shall receive mercy.	1 … for theirs is the kingdom of heaven.	3 … for they shall inherit the earth.	7 … for they shall be called sons of God.
4 … for they shall be satisfied.	8 …for theirs is the kingdom of heaven.	6 …for they shall see God.	2 …for they shall be comforted.

5 Mother Mary	1 Nathanael	3 Little James & Thaddeus	4 Big James & John
8 John the Baptist & Matthew	6 Mary, Ramah, and Thomas	2 Andrew	7 Philip, Simon, and Zee